Spiritual Real Estate

A JUNGIAN JOURNEY
Find Own and Develop your Inner Properties

Joanne Park

KV
Kentwood Village Press
Los Angeles Ca

Joanne Park/Kentwood Village Press
9100 S. Sepulveda Blvd. #127
Los Angeles Ca. 90045
www.JoannePark.com

Book Layout by diypublishing.co.nz
Author's photo: Douglas Castleman
Cover Art: I stock photos

Spiritual Real Estate/Joanne Park. -- 1st ed.
Print Edition ISBN 978-0-6927568-2-9
Kindle Edition ISBN 978-0-692756

Dedication

To my husband Kenneth
who has both inspired me and shared
the dream and the journey

ACKNOWLEDGMENTS

To Russell Lockhart, my guide and steady hand for many years; My wonderful fellow writers and critique group, Deborah Glik, Katherine Sartori, Mary Terzian, Rebecca Stahl, Sue Perry and Lynn Schubert, whose support kept me going, Editors; Jenny Jensen, and my dear friend and voice of encouragement Jeff Larsen, and to Carl Gustav Jung, but for whom there would be no book.

Contents

Introduction

"I am not what happened to me, I am what I choose to become". (Jung)

I am an ordinary woman attempting to live an extra-ordinary life with the knowledge that, though life is short, it is also wide and deep.

After many years working as a Real Estate broker and helping people to find properties in the outer world, I have learned that finding, owning, and de-veloping our inner properties is of far greater importance. My purpose for writing this book is to inspire readers to live more conscious, fully awake lives, by learning to gain access to the wealth of the hidden real estate within.

This book is based on the psychological system and life's work of Swiss psychologist, Carl Gustav Jung, whose insights continue to resonate and gain value with each new generation.

There are available today volumes upon volumes of Jung's work and many scholarly books written about him. The problem for myself, and others, has been, the complexity of the writing; one might need to have specialized training to apply the valuable prin-ciples to their lives. My effort here is to make the material accessible to everyone.

1

When I discovered Jung's psychology I was at one of the lowest points in my life. Trapped in a loveless, destructive marriage, filled with self-loathing, depression, and feeling out of control in many areas of life, I found my way in the 1970s to a "touchy-feely" group therapy session in Southern California, where I live.

The therapist leading the group immediately attracted me. He was young and handsome and that was enough to win my interest. After the group meeting we talked and he agreed to take me on as a private patient. He told me he was a Jungian. I had no idea what that was but he was so good-looking and I was so lost it sounded good to me.

After only a few sessions together he left the state, but he referred me to the Jung Institute in Los Angeles and I soon found myself in therapy with a brilliant and compassionate analyst. I learned Jungian psychotherapy, which goes much deeper than counseling, consists of an analyst and an analysand (me). I knew nothing at the beginning. I didn't get the connection between my dreams and my life, my pain and my ego, but I did find that the weekly sessions with my analyst and the dream journal I began to keep were acting like bulldozers, breaking up and moving around the many pieces of the personal puzzle deep within me.

Something mysterious was happening. A pinhole of light started shining through to the dark side of life where I had resided. The dreams I previously thought of as nightmares turned into gifts as they pointed the way to the land of my Shadow, that hidden part of me living in my unconscious, which contained the parts of me I'd chosen not to include in my idea of who I was. Admittedly, this was scary. I had perfectly good reasons to reject these perceived character "flaws" in the first place. I didn't realize when I discarded them they didn't leave me, but instead went "underground".

While a surprising number of people have never heard of Jung, they have heard of some the words he gave life and meaning to. The most familiar of these are: Introvert, Extrovert, do you know which you are? Maybe both? Archetype, the images found all around us that represent the properties within; Ego, the "I" we are; Shadow, the hidden, rejected part of ourselves; Persona, the face we present to the public; Synchronicity, the meaningful coincidences in our life; Transcendence, our psychological transformation; and Individuation, the process that leads to a reunion with the Self, our true heart. Individuation represents the final step to becoming the person we are meant to be.

Now, after a lifetime of increased understanding of myself and others, there lives within me a Wise Old Woman and a Wise Old Man. As these two grow stronger they do not want to feel their hard-earned wisdom is all for nothing. In a society that reveres youth, they feel displaced. They go quietly through our days together observing a world at war, families torn apart by divorce, and violence toward Self and others as prevalent as a cold. They feel compelled to make sense out of the senseless, to spread light into the darkness. They live in me, and I, being the ordinary woman I am, need to let them speak out.

I would feel helpless and hopeless if it were not for these wisdom figures and other properties I have come to know and own, such as the Heroine, the Compassionate One, the One who Doesn't Quit, the Shadow that understands and recognizes evil, and the deep Self that regulates my inner universe. Without these helpers and more, I would be sitting in a heap at the mouth of a very dark cave, disheveled, hungry, homeless, with dried tears on my dirt-streaked face. This was an early dream image of mine, before I started my journey into the territory of the unconscious.

Thankfully, I have discovered these inner partners and they are the properties, called by Jung, the Archetypes. They are the birthright of every human being.

I wrote this book to introduce the concept of inner properties/Archetypes so readers may choose to undertake the journey to find, own, and develop those properties, which await discovery within each of us.

In these pages I will provide the information and tools to start you on your way to the goal of Individuation, which occurs when we have successfully integrated the hidden properties into our consciousness, thereby leading to a transformation and a realization of our true Self and the experience of wholeness that, like me, you will treasure.

Part One

Preparing
The Way

One

What Do You Mean I'm Not Conscious?

"Until you make the unconscious conscious, it will direct your life and you will call it fate." (Jung 1965)

There are many people who are only partially conscious. Even among absolutely civilized Europeans there are a disproportionately high number of individuals who spend a great part of their lives in an abnormally unconscious state. They know what happens to them, but they do not know what they do or say. They cannot judge the consequences of their actions. These are people who are abnormally unconscious, that is, in a primitive state. What then finally makes them conscious? If they get a slap in the face, then they become conscious: something really happens, and that makes them conscious.
(Jung 1934)

I still remember when a friend told me I was un-conscious which caused me to question her status as a friend. I have since learned to appreciate her in-put. At that time though I had already survived an almost fatal illness, was unhappily married, and was just beginning my adventure in Jungian analysis. I thought I knew a lot and only needed a slight tweak-ing, a quick fix from my analyst and that would be that. Of course I was perpetually unhappy, and cer-tain the fault belonged to my husband my parents, my job, God.

But instead I found that I was unconscious as I blundered along making the same mistakes over and over again. I also discovered that consciousness is mysterious, elusive, and often a burden. Ignorance can be blissful and ignorance is unconsciousness. After all, how much easier it is to blame others for all that goes wrong in our lives than to become aware we may be contributing to our own problems.

It's understandable to believe we are conscious when we're not. At any given waking moment we are aware of what we are doing and saying. What we are not aware of is why we do what we do and say what we say; why we react to others as we do, and act out in ways that seem to be against our will, severely limiting our responsibility and control over our lives.

The consciousness Jung talked about occurs when we realize that what we are aware of in the moment is but a miniature picture of our reality, a small piece of landmass visible above the vast ocean of the unconscious. Until we begin to explore the contents of all that is hidden from view we can never lead a conscious, purposeful and fully competent life. Strange as it sounds we become more conscious the more we realize we are not. When we live our lives on automatic pilot, blaming others for all that is wrong with the world and ourselves, repeating mistakes over and over again, and feeling empty and incapable of fulfillment, we are unconscious.

Consciousness is not an item like a pair of shoes that once bought can be kept forever. Our conscious awareness of ourselves is always changing and we have multiple reasons for resisting new information. To live a conscious life is a burden because we don't want to know we are at fault and need to change. It might be inconvenient, too much work, threatening to our ego, just plain uncomfortable to see the truth. It's so much easier not to know.

But when we linger too long in an unconscious existence, something will generally happen to shake us awake. The more unconscious we are, the greater the magnitude of the jolt.

I personally have gone through accident-prone periods of life where I've tripped, fallen flat on my face, bumped my head, cut a finger, burned myself and after the second or third of these types of so-called accidents in a short amount of time, I suddenly got it. My unconscious mind was trying its hardest to get my attention. I sometimes have to be literally hit on the head to realize I need to stop what I'm doing and tune in and turn up the volume so I can hear the message being given to me. Nearly always I have gotten out of balance in a serious way.

Jung called this one-sidedness. This can happen when a thinking person spends too much time in his head and not enough in his feelings, or when an intuitive person loses touch with the here and now while chasing one new adventure after another. Sometimes it's a wake-up call to an inflated ego. Signals also come from our relationships, which often go wrong as we slip out of consciousness.

Bodily symptoms are excellent ways for the unconscious to speak to us. In the absence of actual medical issues, difficulty swallowing could force one to ask what in life can't you swallow. Back pain often is a sign of carrying too heavy a load. Lumps in ones throat can mean unshed tears.

Most frequently the messages are delivered at night while we sleep. Our dreams are a direct link to the unconscious. Some don't take them seriously, but the more we dismiss our dream messages, the more insistent the unconscious may become in getting our attention. People who go a lifetime ignoring all the signals generally have a high price to pay in serious illness, accidents, or just unhappy and unfulfilled lives and relationships.

There are two kinds of unconscious mind, the personal and the collective. Our personal unconscious contains everything that happens to us every day, along with all we don't want to know about ourselves, and all there is not enough room for in our conscious mind. Every time we struggle to recall a name the personal unconscious goes to work. Who has not had the experience of having the name suddenly pop into our consciousness uncovered and delivered by the unconscious? Nothing is ever lost when it comes to our personal existence.

The collective unconscious, on the other hand, belongs to everyone. This is the ocean connecting us to each other, from one culture to another, generation after generation.

The contents of the collective unconscious come to us in the form of myths, dreams, religious symbols, fairy tales, and archetypal images. The messages coming from here are often meant to compensate for the one-sidedness, the suffering, and the anxieties of mankind in general - hunger, war, disease, old age, and death. The symbols may be common to all, but they evolve in individual cultures differently. For example, the image of hero is common to all people and lives in the collective unconscious, yet the martyred Jihadist hero is a far cry from Superman of the western world. The spin of a culture can substantially change the way in which the image manifests in the world.

A majority of our dreams come from the personal unconscious where we are working out many of our daily life problems; we dream of our families, our jobs, our mental and physical states. Then one day comes a "big" dream, an archetypal dream, one we don't easily, if ever, forget. This dream often signals a change in our psyche, a new way of being that may not become apparent for years.

By keeping a dream journal I was able to see how these seeds of new perspective began to be manifested in my life. The images in these dreams are not only beyond our daily lives but are so foreign we often must look them up to know what their origin might be. (Detail on dreams is found later in chapter fourteen.)

In this book I suggest that everyone has a pathway that leads to ownership of the properties that live in the unconscious. We each own a personal unconscious exclusively, while the collective unconscious is more like a condominium community. We can own a unit but we are still a part of the whole and it's the welfare of the whole property that is at stake as we become conscious. I think of the many condominium owners who never attend a single board meeting, yet complain constantly at how poorly things are run.

The images we receive through our dreams are often symbolic, representing something other than they appear. Where these symbols originated is still debated. Marie-Louise von Franz, noted Swiss Jungian Psychologist, scholar, and close associate of Jung, in Man and his Symbols, states, "Often they sprang from one person's personal unconscious and made their way into the cultural psyche."

But not under debate is the fact these symbols exist. Heroes and heroines, mothers, fathers, dragons and crosses, gods and goddesses, serpents and demons alike – all live in the collective unconscious. A question often asked is why these images still take on mythological forms even in the modern secular world. An answer coming from deep in our collective unconscious is that human life has always been a journey and often a struggle and these archetypal symbols from the ancient past are just as meaningful and relevant today in helping us to understand where we are going and why.

There are times in history where people have been lured into a kind of hypnosis and rather than living from their own consciousness they fall into the realm of a collective consciousness. This is seen often within groups of people who all share common beliefs and life style and is easily recognizable by a scripted kind of speech. All the members of the group speak almost in a monotone with the same words spoken by all members. I think today they are called "talking points." I personally go on the alert the minute I am in the presence of a group consciousness and group speak, lest I get lulled out of my own personal consciousness.

There may never be a greater example than that of the Nazi party, which caused otherwise good people in Germany to take on the images of the super race which sprang in part from Adolph Hitler's personal unconscious and grew into a national collective consciousness. This mass movement to eradicate the Jew and the five million others, mostly Poles, Serbs and anyone Hitler considered deviant or threatening, gained support in many quarters. Those who did not join in often chose to stay unaware. Only when the world was slapped in the face by Hitler's goal of world domination did people begin to wake up. As the evil became more consciously recognized by even the participants, the spell of Hitler's megalomania began to break. People woke as if from a stupor because a generation had been living in a collective consciousness of evil and to this day the world remains hard pressed to explain how Hitler was able to pull this off. It was as if the world went to sleep.

It is imperative for the survival of mankind that we stay personally conscious enough to discern when we are in jeopardy of being put to sleep in this way. By learning to seek out and develop the inner properties of our personal and collective unconscious as well as recognizing the collective consciousness of groups that choose to shut out all which is different, threatening, scary, and unknown we will be taking the first steps toward conscious living.

Be encouraged that the most frightening images we face can quickly lose their fierceness and their hold over us through knowing them. While working as a Travelers Aid at the airport I was put on alert for terrorists. Pictures had been circulated and I was on edge as I watched each person passing by. I saw a man whose appearance was suspicious. He had a dark swarthy look, seemed highly anxious, and wore a dour expression. I was about to call security when a person brought me a found wallet and airline tickets. I stopped to page the name in the wallet and within moments my "potential terrorist" appeared at my desk. He was toothless and grinning, with tears in his eyes as he reached across my desk to hug me and to be reunited with his wallet. All my previous images evaporated. I am now more wary of my snap decisions and judgments of people and situations.

There are mysteries surrounding consciousness, and unconsciousness, which I will never solve for myself, and the debates and studies continue today. What I do know from experience is once I woke up, even a little, to the fact "I" my ego was not alone, that there exists within me abundant properties to explore and bring into my conscious awareness, my life changed for the better. My fears abated, my relationships improved, and my growth as an evolved human took giant steps.

Two

What is an Inner Property and Why Should I Own it?

Many know what an Archetype is, they just don't know they know. Books, myths, movies and all of life are full of them. What greater recent archetype of The Wizard than Harry Potter. He also is an amazing Child /Hero archetype. Children and adults alike find Harry fascinating. The King, the Ogre, the Prince and Princess found in fairy tales and movies are all common archetypes we meet early in life. Our fascination with them is a clue that these images are meaningful.

Jung discovered these outward symbols also exist within each of us and the stronger our connection to them, the more alive they are in our unconscious.

Ask yourself Who dwells within you? The Trickster? The Artist? The Lover? The Prostitute?

(Remember *Pretty Woman*) A Miser? (Who doesn't love to hate Scrooge)? A Messiah?

An example, which has touched many, is the recent phenomenal success of the movie *"Frozen"*. Anna, a fearless and daring optimist, teams up with Rugged Mountain Man, to find her sister, the regal Elsa, who is trapped in eternal winter and hiding her inner fear. Through Anna she comes to realize that love can conquer fear and she now has what a family's love can give her: happiness. All the little girls I know resonated completely with the child/heroines presented in this film.

Have you ever needed the help of Fearless Optimist to get through a tough patch of life? Wouldn't you love to call up Rugged Mountain Man when you need him?

And what of the enduring *Star Wars* characters and our fascination with them? This powerful continuing story represents the ultimate battle of light against dark, good versus evil, and death and rebirth. The amazing Hero we all wish to be, Luke Skywalker, whose quest to defeat the dark side and save princess Leia leaves us breathless.

The dark and sinister Darth Vader represents for us our own dark natures while the purity and goodness of Princess Leia lives in us as well. And the wisdom of Obi-Wan Kenobi is forever a worthy goal for us mortals.

When we are confronted with someone needing help and we step in, the archetype of the Hero or the Rescuer has been summoned. When we comfort a crying child, the Mother archetype in us is present and when we rage out of control at another, our dark side has been touched. We just are not consciously aware of what is going on.

To consciously find and recognize these properties and own them, makes us able to call on them independently. This is the path that enables us to experience our own power and to become Self-Reliant. In Jungian terms, this leads to Individuation, the goal of becoming a whole, differentiated person.

In Jung's practice with a wide variety of patients from all over the world and even his work with schizophrenics, he kept noticing common recurring themes coming from their unconscious. This led him to his theory of the Archetypes. What was this common link between us all? The search for this answer continued for the rest of his life and his findings form the basis of his psychological system.

The word Archetype derives from the Greek *Archetypos* meaning first of its kind. Jung discovered first of their kind patterns living deep in the collective unconscious and representing the patterns from which every human personality is derived. These Archetype/Properties belong to all of us, and are ever available to be owned and enhanced in all the ways our instincts and imagination can offer.

Over the course of my career in Real Estate I have sold hundreds of homes. This is what I know about them. They all have walls, floors, roofs and ceilings, doors to enter by and windows to look out of. Whether they are 500 square feet or 5,000, a teepee, an igloo or a tent - even a Quonset hut, which I once lived in - they start out with these basic features, which represent the universal pattern for all houses.

Home is an Archetype that exists deep within our unconscious and the urge to have a home is an abiding human instinct. In fact, the house has become the symbol of the psyche in Jung's work.

As a Real Estate Agent I have never been in any two houses that are alike, even in a tract of hundreds, once the owner has applied their individual images. Even the basic pattern is enhanced. Walls and ceilings, doors and windows vary in height and thickness, color, texture, and design. The shape and size of a house is always evolving, but throughout the centuries the original pattern remains. So it is in the world. Even as each person expresses the archetypes in their own unique way, they are all derived from the same set of plans.

Although I will include here the main Archetypal Properties Jung introduced to the world, in meeting them we cannot help but bump into some of the hundreds of others one meets in life.

If you will, imagine the collective unconscious as a giant sea upon which we each are a floating island, connected to each other by the water beneath and around us. Within this ocean of the unconscious lies all the major patterns/properties, which give form and expression to every human activity.

In order to access these properties, our ego must begin a heroic journey - heroic because it takes courage and sacrifice. Until the journey begins our ego is the center of our universe. In other words, the "I" we go through life as – our name, job, status and idea of ourselves. The sacrifice involved comes through realizing and accepting that there might be more to us than just this ego and the relinquishing of its power in our life.

Since the ego does not relish giving up its position as number one, the distance to the new venture can be enormous. Usually a crisis in life needs to occur to push our ego over the edge, some sign of weakness - an event that causes the ego to earnestly doubt itself, before it willingly searches for help from within.

First, however, the ego must become aware that there exists a place to journey toward. Until then, Ego believes itself to be like the sun, with all other properties circling around it. (In 1632, Italian scientist Galileo was tried by the Inquisition, found "vehemently suspect of heresy" and spent the remaining nine years of his life under house arrest for suggesting the sun, rather than the earth, was the center of the universe.)

The first awareness that our ego might be just one of many properties revolving around something greater than itself often does not arise until midlife. That's when a vague memory of a greater Self, the birthplace of the ego, begins to break through. As Jung described the process, "The first half of life is devoted to forming a healthy ego. The second half is going inward and letting go of it."

In the first half of life we don a mask, called by Jung, Persona. The mask represents the person we wish others to think we are and even if our masks do not agree with who we really are, we seem able to handle the differences pretty well.

One way we do this is to repress those things about ourselves, whether positive or negative, which do not fit the person we think we are. We do this by casting them into the unconscious where they take up residence as our Shadow, one of the first properties we must retrieve. These cast off parts have not left us, they have just dropped out of our conscious minds.

Eventually this mode of living stops working. By midlife the mask we wear may be so developed it is literally stuck to us and cannot be removed even though we are exhausted from carrying the weight and our true selves are lost. Our lives have narrowed along with our choices and relationships, which continually must fit our image of who we are, the mask we wear. This is often the signal when the ego needs to ask:

Is that all there is?

This common question is the one that launches the journey inward. It can happen when we no longer feel satisfied with the things our ego has achieved and accumulated for us, when emptiness creeps in no matter how much we have attained in the world, and the person we are is not the person we wish to be. That's when we are ready to begin our journey to the properties within our unconscious, which are ready and waiting to enter into a relationship with us. As Jung described it:

> *I have frequently seen people become neurotic when they content themselves with inadequate or wrong answers to the questions of life. They seek position, marriage, reputation, outward success or money, and remain unhappy and neurotic even when they have attained what they were seeking. Such people are usually confined to too narrow a spiritual horizon. Their life has not sufficient content, sufficient meaning. If they are enabled to develop into more spacious personalities, the neurosis generally disappears. (Jung 1965)*

Bill W., founder of Alcoholic's Anonymous, often credited Jung as the inspiration of the organization and cited the following statement by Jung. "If you substitute the word "alcoholic" for "neurotic," it expresses how A.A. works; but it applies to everyone."

In this writing you will meet The Shadow, The Persona, The Anima, The Animus, The Wise Old Woman and Man, and the parent of them all, The Self. But many other archetypes are waiting to be discovered. Only a few of which are: the beggar, the lover, the mother, the child, the father, the devil, the saint, the sinner, the savior and the trickster. These patterns of human behavior reside in the collective unconscious and are expressed in the world only through human beings.

Another way to recognize archetypes is when they become headlines internationally. Eve"nts or people that touch, fascinate and captivate the public speak to a strong archetypal quality. Fascination is a sure sign that an archetype in the collective unconscious has been stirred.

The death of "The Crocodile Hunter" Steve Irwin in 2006 was such an archetype. The poisonous barb of a stingray killed him while filming a documentary. Known as a "wildlife warrior" a daredevil around dangerous beasts, he took risks constantly on television, right in front of a worldwide audience of two hundred million. He represented to the world the archetype of supreme risk taker and daredevil adventurer. He expressed the part of us that flies in the face of danger. Few of us get to live out this archetype in our daily lives and so Steve Irwin did it for us.

We thought him to be immortal and were shocked by his death for he was the property in us representing our immortality.

Another person who has become recognized as an archetype is Anne Frank, holocaust heroine who in the face of deepest danger and despair was able to keep her spirit alive. Also, Helen Keller, a woman unable to see, speak or hear, who was victorious against all odds and had the will to live in spite of the toughest obstacles.

We do not have to battle deadly beasts or suffer the deprivations of Frank and Keller to access these aspects of risk-taking, fearlessness, and supreme strength in the face of adversity. The risks we take and the heroism we show can be as accessible as making necessary changes in our lives, entering into relationships, and pursuing our dreams. The survivor in us can express itself daily, as we meet our problems and obstacles head on and do not give up.

The more we become conscious of these archetypal properties within ourselves and the more we give expression to them in our individual lives, the closer we are to becoming whole.

But be forewarned before these properties are made conscious; our threatened egos may act out in hurtful and counterproductive ways. As an example: a perfectionist will be easily irritated and irrationally upset by any sign of imperfection. Until the ego owns the property of flawed human, this person will be hard to live with and will suffer consequences. A major and almost fatal error may have to occur before this person will undertake the journey inward.

Meanwhile, these properties of the unconscious are not lying dormant, but in fact may possess us and act out through us even if we do not own them. The "accidents" and "mistakes" made by the perfectionist are such a possession. Who was not shocked when perfectionist Martha Stewart landed in jail?

It comes down to a decision to either consciously choose the life we were meant to live or live the life chosen only by our egos. The freedom to choose comes through conscious awareness. As we further explore the archetypes and learn how these inner properties work in us, and what they want from us, we become empowered to use their enormous energies in ways that enhance our existence and bring us closer to wholeness.

If we never see there is more to ourselves than our egos, we will unlikely gain any ground toward Individuation, the goal set forth by Jung. An ego alone is too flimsy and vulnerable to accomplish the job.

Through an ongoing acquaintanceship with all the archetypal properties belonging to us we move far beyond a two-dimensional life. As we explore these energies we will reacquaint with the properties that made early appearances in our life such as the child artist, athlete, or intellectual. Did these energies materialize or were they relegated to the shadow? Our early adult years brought further energies that fueled our dreams and ambitions. Did we manifest them? Only as we take active ownership of the many archetype/properties available to us can we successfully travel through the second half of life becoming conscious, sturdy, and wise enough to achieve the goal of Individuation and the longed-for meeting up with our Self.

Suggested Exercise.

It can be illuminating to make a list of the Archetypes that have acted upon you in your life. Are you aware of them? Are you controlled by any one of them? Have you repressed or ignored them?

Included in the Appendix of the book is a list of many suggested properties. Feel free to add to it. Looking through the list, choose all that speak to you both positively and negatively.

All Archetypes can be used positively when we are aware of them or impact negatively when they live in the shadows. For example, The Storyteller may inspire the world with wonderful stories or if that archetype stays hidden, become a liar. The Mother archetype can be a truly loving, unconditionally nurturing mother or if repressed, a mother capable of doing great harm to her children.

Doing this exercise, allow enough time. Take days, weeks or longer. Your list at first might be quite long. From the ones you choose, begin to whittle the list to your top six or eight. Make sure to add to those a couple of negative ones.

Sit with each of these chosen Archetypes and approach it as a new acquaintance in your life. Question it. When did you first appear in my life? How are you expressed? Ask its value to you or the harm it is doing? Use your imagination.

Choose ways to work with these selected images. Put a face to them, what do they look like? How do they dress, where do they live? Invite them to dinner, strike up a conversation, place them in situations, especially ones familiar to you: how do they act? When owned consciously they can be a positive influence in the world. While they remain in the shadow land they can do much damage. Even the Bully, once conscious, can protect you from the bully within you that's constantly beating you up. Befriend the archetypes that speak loudest to you. Make use of their amazing powers.

These Archetypes will shine the light on your soul and help you to use their energies and/or reclaim them from your shadow, I offer a partial example of my own original list, which I then slimmed down to the four most important, and added two more that I rescued from the shadow land so they can now help me rather than harm me.

The Busy Professional; The Social Planner; The Problem Solver; The Seductress; The Organizer; The Spiritual Advisor; The Nag; The Good Neighbor; The Judge; The Volunteer; The Critic; The Rebel; The Know-It-All; The Mother. I could go on with many more. These are all Patterns of properties that speak to my life. I have rescued the critic and the nag from a life in the shadows to help me write this book.

Three

Getting Started

We live life much like we drive our vehicles, in automatic most of the time. Every few years the state calls upon us to take a driver's test. We rush off to the DMV for the rulebook and never fail to be surprised at how little of the rules we have remembered. We must brush up on the old ones while learning a few new ones.

In life, we seldom have the advantage of studying the rulebook before we are tested. It usually happens the other way around. We are tested and then we begin to look for the rules. While most learn early to obey the obvious laws of the society we live in, many remain in the dark regarding the laws that govern our inner lives. We graduate High School with the barest of information of the world we are entering and zero information as to the workings or our psyche/soul.

Yet no shortage of books are available, the greatest in western society being the Holy Bible. We also can learn from an abundance of priests, ministers, rabbis, psychologists, psychiatrists, and more recently accepted, channelers, astrologers, psychics, healers, shamans, body-workers, etc. This plethora of teachers certainly points to a need on the part of humanity to be guided in the ways of their inner lives.

So why do so many sincerely striving people continue to wander spiritually? I suggest that one reason is that we are not willing to learn *how to fish*. We try instead to buy the fish, all cleaned and fileted, from a fisherman who often just bought his own fish from someone else. An old Chinese proverb says "Give a man a fish and you feed him for a day. Teach a man to fish and you feed him for a lifetime."

Starving people must be taught to get their own food. Loving teachers can teach them how. This means a teacher must be more than his ego, for an ego can never teach this lesson of self-reliance. It calls for much restraint and generosity on the part of the teacher. The rules to the inner world are available but it takes willingness on our part to provide for ourselves.

Therefore, our noble task through life is to learn the way to the fishing hole so we may begin to catch all we need to become the whole person we are meant to be. This requires not just searching out and finding our inner properties, but also acknowledging and taking responsibility for what we discover, so we can change, become stronger, progress and begin to expand on the basic idea of what a human is.

Jung called this process *differentiation,* meaning a conscious separation of our inner properties, one from each other, so we can learn to recognize and use them independently in our lives. Just as our embryonic cells are identical upon conception, we are only fully born nine months later after the specific tissues develop (differentiate) into bone, heart, muscle, and skin.

The journey begins with an ego, which I will define here as the everyday person we are consciously — one with some awareness, no matter how vague, that there is more to life than what it sees and touches and knows. An ego that senses something un-seeable, untouchable, and unknowable; something ego reluctantly must admit is larger than itself, or at least outside its immediate awareness.

At puberty we are moving away from total dependence as our egos begin to fully emerge. Our bodies are developing and our first major awareness of ourselves as different from other selves, self-consciousness, emerges right along with our budding breasts and genitals. These bodily changes are like the guns at the starting gate. Fueled by hormones and incredibly high energy, we step boldly off the precipice into a life whose object is unclear and whose rules are a mystery. A great deal of anxiety is understandably part of this process.

This early stage of the journey is essential for our ego, which is the property that gets us our stuff: our money, our positions, and our identity in the world. This stage of life, led by the ego, can last well into the first three decades of life and even beyond.

Up to this time, our egos have acted as the guardians of the person we have become, represented by our name, social security number, our clever email address, our twitter handles, our jobs, our families, what we think, what we do, and who we are in the world.

But as other aspects of our being — our inner properties — begin to struggle out of unconsciousness, and fight to have life and relationship, our ego must let down its guard and welcome the newcomers. As a natural occurrence our ego may become threatened and unwittingly open the door from the unconscious that causes us to act out in ways hurtful and counterproductive to our growth. Only if we are willing and able to see what our ego is up to can we withstand the assault.

Possession

One example comes from a close friend who was on the brink of moving from a life in the shadows to one offering much opportunity and success, but then he walked out of a major department store with an armful of un-purchased clothing and of course was caught immediately. This person had never stolen a thing in his life and was horrified. His ego had become so threatened by the new life presenting itself it sabotaged his future.

What is going on here? Surely we don't want to sabotage our lives. Have you ever said to yourself, "I don't know what got into me," or "the devil made me do it"? I can assure you there were times in my life when I felt I needed an exorcism. A so-called "mood" would take me over and spoil the best of times for me. More than once I have said, "I don't know what made me do that or I don't know what made me say that." These are huge hints that an archetype/property has taken over our ego and is acting out without our willingness. We have, in fact, lost our free will at that time. Jung referred to this takeover by the archetypes as a *Complex.* In Real Estate lingo, we have been taken over by eminent domain.

You may be familiar with the following terms: inferiority complex, Napoleon complex, Mother complex Father complex, Power complex, Superman complex, Cinderella, Don Juan, Messiah, Madonna-prostitute. These are just a few of the complexes that can take us over and interfere in our lives. I would be surprised if you haven't known people in your life that you could quickly identify as having one of these complexes.

Before these archetypes reach this level of occupation in our lives they most likely had previously tried to get our attention through our dreams and fantasies. If we do not stop at those times and ask ourselves what is going on, (this is not me) and search deeper for an answer, they will become our total mode of operation.

A person with a power complex becomes a "control freak." The one with an inferiority complex will never feel adequate in the world. As long as we remain unconscious to these properties, and they have their way with us, the world is fully aware and sees them in operation. It is we who are the last to know, for we have truly become possessed. It's like one of my favorite old science fiction movies, The Invasion of The Body Snatchers and I'm sure, to a person, you have experienced some moments of being body snatched.

We all have complexes. Actually the word complex comes from the Latin *complectere*, and it means, "to embrace." And actually they are our friends when we can do this. These are the helpers when we are consciously aware of them, and can use them when we need them. They only possess us as long as we deny their existence. To quote Jung, "The Via Regia [royal road] to the unconscious, however, is not the dream...but the complex, which is the author of dreams and of symptoms."

With our 24/7 news/gossip coverage we are more privy to witness publicly the possession of others. In 2014 it appeared that many of the Secret Service in

Washington DC, chosen to guard the president, were "possessed" as they became drunk and sexually active on duty.

And one shocking example of possession was the 2015 story of Rachel Dolezal, the former NAACP chapter president, who was born to white parents. She presented herself as an African-American woman and, to the frustration of many, continued to claim in interviews in light of the scandal that she identified as black. Her initial public denial of being white rather than just acknowledging her true strong empathy and caring for black people (a complex including the archetype of the black woman that possessed her) in the end severely damaged her credibility.

Complexes are formed by a group of archetypes combining. An example of a positive complex can be found in former, beloved UCLA coach John Wooden. All his players to a man viewed him as a father figure. He obviously had a strong, conscious, Father Archetype, but to account for his great success it must have combined with other strong Archetypes; perhaps Winner, Teacher, Tough Man, Inspirer. He loved his players but was always firm. He taught them discipline, teamwork, and lessons in being men.

Four

The Shadow

The descent begins

Waking in the night from a nightmare, heart pounding, body sweaty, remnants of a meeting with dirty, dangerous, and frightening characters in slums, dark deserted streets, falling down houses, back alleys, you can be sure you have stumbled into the territory of the shadow. The rocky, cavernous, terrain is hard to traverse. The air is often thick and polluted. The environment may resemble a scene in a horror movie. Franz in The Process of Individuation says, "The shadow may appear in dreams and visions in various forms, and typically appears as a person of the same sex as that of the dreamer."

This property, waiting discovery and development, is one of the most dangerous and powerful we will ever encounter while at the same time the most beneficial once we own it. It is the source of the best and the worst in all of us. It is the all-important first step toward individuation.

According to Jolande Jacobi in her book The Way of Individuation, she says:

> *"the confrontation with the shadow and its integration must always be achieved first in the individuation process, in order to strengthen the ego for further laps in the journey and for the crucial encounter with the Self. That is why the shadow qualities must first be made conscious, even at the risk of neglecting other aspects and other figures presented by the psychic material."*

Ego and shadow are a potent partnership of opposites, which once united have the power to take on the archetypes within.

In the book *C.G. Jung Speaking*, Jung was said to tell of a distinguished man he once met, a Quaker, who could not imagine that he had ever done anything wrong in his life. "And do you know what happened to his children?" Jung asked:

> *The son became a thief and the daughter a prostitute. Because the father would not take on his shadow, his share in the imperfection of human nature, his children were compelled to live out the dark side, which he had ignored. (Jung and Reich 1977)*

We've heard of the minister's son who burns down the church and the teetotaler who raises an alcoholic.

The shadow is the essential property that must be owned before a person can come into their full humanity and wholeness, for it represents our repressed, disowned and pushed away nature that once discovered and reclaimed by us turns into, not only our greatest ally, but also ally to our friends and loved ones; our enemies; our communities, and especially the world. This is the one property that can transform our personality out of flatness and lack of vigor into a vital, creative, fully alive human being. We often begin our journey to the shadow during a period of depression, boredom, and general malaise.

My first dream encounter with my shadow took place at the mouth of a cave. There sat a shabby, dirty, crying young girl. I walked right by her without asking what her problem was or if I could help. Gradually as I worked my way deeper on my journey and into the cave, I came to recognize this girl as my shadow and as a result I became able to own this property and finally to accept the shabby, dirty, needy part of myself which I had long ignored and disowned, and instead I began to comfort and take care of her. This changed my life.

While this shadow property languishes in the unconscious, it is far from vacant. The unauthorized tenants we encounter here are an incredible and motley assortment. Their true natures are always disguised and they often appear as drug dealers, burglars, terrorists, prostitutes, witches, and/or souls acting out our animal nature. Elements from nature are also alive in our shadows; water, fire, air, earth, and animals are also represented.

A very important dream for me continued to recur. This signals an important message trying to come through to the conscious mind. In the dream, a dog approached me, gnarling and threatening, and each time I shook myself awake, heart pounding, in sheer terror of being bitten. The nightmare continued over a period of several months until one night, instead of waking myself in fear, I allowed the dog to approach. As he opened his mouth and closed it on my arm, in place of the terrible bite I anticipated, the dog turned into a playful puppy and the bite into a gentle touch.

Following this dream, with the help of my analyst, and my own work, I discovered the dog was the symbol for my instinctual nature, which I had severely repressed. This dream became a major gift to me, for I was then able to trust my instincts rather than continue to fear them.

While we predominately discard these dark aspects to the shadow land, it is not impossible to see generous, warm, loving, intelligent, creative, enthusiastic, and open tenants, who also have been unable to find a permanent conscious home in our psyches. This is very common in those with low self-esteem. It is just as easy to repress our positive traits as the negative ones. Any unlived and unrecognized part of us can be relegated to the shadow property.

I cannot help but wonder about the murdering young man who walked into a South Carolina Church, sat among the praying parishioners, and then cold bloodily killed nine of those parishioners. If he could see his shadow, would it be good, pious, and saintly? Had he so repressed and rejected that part of himself that he became driven to project it on to these good people and in this way violently kill it? This is the extreme danger and power of the unrecognized shadow.

We can try not to notice this property for many years, pushing it away, happy to project it onto others which means that what we accuse others of we don't accept in ourselves. This can damage many relationships. But thankfully the shadow is as persistent as it is powerful in getting our attention.

As Jung explains, "How can I be substantial if I do not cast a shadow? I must have a dark side also if I am to be whole."

Owning the shadow property comes by no longer ignoring its existence and by assuming full responsibility for it. This requires doing the maintenance, keeping the lights on, and the water of consciousness flowing through it.

The relationship with our shadow needs to continue throughout our lives for we are never free of the desire to disown parts of ourselves. But through consciousness we are able to more quickly identify the shadow part and reclaim it, like a good real estate "flipper" rehabilitating a derelict property. It is very profitable to our spirit.

While our shadow remains unconscious everything dark and evil is thought to be outside of us and of course if this were true there would be nothing to do about it. This is why so many people live in fear with a great sense of helplessness. But once the decision to own the shadow property is made and the lights of consciousness get turned on, the darkness has a face, and that face can turn from monstrous to loving. It is equivalent to purchasing a slum property only to have it become beachfront.

I recently witnessed a two–year-old discovering a patch of light splashing across a hardwood floor. His delight was palpable. He gingerly placed a foot into the light and then put both feet firmly on the spot. Squealing with joy he ran to the dark side of the floor. "Light, dark, light, and dark" he shrieked, laughing. What a discovery. How effortlessly the toddler recognizes these places. If only as mature adults we could so easily and visibly acknowledge the differences and integrate the light and dark aspects of our personalities.

Instead we spend lifetimes relegating our unwanted parts into the dumpster of the shadow property. We think we are clever to be able to ignore our unwanted parts and we go merrily walking through life only on the streets we are comfortable on, unaware the only reason we don't see the shadow is because it has leapt upon our backs as we passed it by and we can't see it. Like kittens hiding their heads behind a curtain and thinking they are invisible, we assume no one else sees our shadow. Not so. It is clearly visible to others as it clings fast to us, its weight pulling us down.

The persistent nature of the shadow won't leave us alone no matter how hard we try to hide from it. It begins to haunt our sleep, appearing in dreams. When we cannot stand the discomfort any longer we hurl it off of our backs in the direction of some other, usually of the same sex. In any event, someone we can identify as capable of wearing it, as they then become the giant movie screen of our life. It is here as master projectionists we put these unwanted parts onto the movie version of life we are viewing. This inevitably leads to a distorted view of life and of the people we interact with. It's like looking at life through funhouse mirrors.

Now the muddle is in full swing. Our shadows, the unwanted, unclaimed parts of ourselves, have attached to the other person and whenever, wherever we encounter that person, or group in the world, their humanity is no longer present, for all we can see is our own shadow in them. This is the kiss of death because by not seeing the true person they are, we are forever kept from becoming our true selves as well.

This may continue for a lifetime. The result is to become reduced to not much more than the mask we wear, having disowned the other parts of ourselves. Our relationships are limited to our comfort zone and our lives become flat and superficial. This treadmill way of living can only be stopped in one way. Reclaim and develop what is rightfully yours.

Transferring Title

When, through crisis, conflict, boredom or just a moment of low resistance, we decide to own the shadow property, we are ready to transfer the title. The number one step is to clearly identify the property.

While the first awareness was through our dreams and the unsavory characters visiting there, a more specific and daily opportunity to identify the property is to look to the person or persons we have projected onto. These are the people we cannot stand, hate, are repulsed by and avoid at all costs, as well as the ones we hold in exalted, exaggerated adoration. These people we hate or love beyond reason are the mirrors, which can be catalyst for retaking our greatest gifts.

An exercise for exposing the projected parts of ourselves is to make a list of those individuals and groups who garner these excessive emotional responses. For each one, write the things about them you detest or love and admire inordinately. When you have finished you will be looking directly into the face of your shadow.

I have an acquaintance, an openly rude and hostile person and I often find myself cringing physically when in her presence. She has been a great help to my life because every time I get that feeling, I take back the shadow part of me that is hostile and rude that I have projected onto her. Granted she is an easy receptacle.

I consider myself a diplomat. I seldom voice my anger in the world. I couch my negative thoughts in the prettiest language, contrary to this woman who makes no bones about her feelings. While I do not aspire to unleash my hostilities upon the world, it is essential I stop repressing them, thereby projecting my cruel, hurtful, and angry side onto others.

Once I owned this shadow property, I was able to love and understand my friend and see that her shadow is her loving self and by example I can now help her to own it, by loving her and encouraging her to reveal her hidden loving nature.

It is natural to fear consciously facing these parts that we have discarded. They are scary. I believed if I expressed my angry feelings they would take me over and I would be out of control, however the opposite is what happened. While my feelings remained unconscious they controlled me. Only by shining the light and taking responsibility for my hostile feelings did I learn how to express my anger constructively and clearly, without resorting to the meanness and rudeness that my friend was stuck with. Once I owned my shadowy anger there was one less person I "couldn't stand" to be with.

I also "hate" stupidity. The word hate is the giveaway that this is my shadow as well. I try continually to repress the knowledge of my own stupidity, preferring instead to project it on to any innocent person able to provide a good container for it. This is usually someone who may not appear to be quick in thought, someone meek and not able to stand up for themselves easily as well as people who are not afraid to appear stupid. They make great containers for any number of projections.

It is not only individuals who have shadows that have been projected outward. Over the history of the world it is easy to see the shadow of nations, races, religions, politicians, and organizations and the terrible destruction caused by their shadows. The anti-Semitism of today has roots in early Christianity and while today many Christians are friends of Judaism and Israel it is because they are reclaiming their shadows.

The initial shadow came about as Christianity (which was born of Judaism) arose in prominence and wanted to separate itself from its Jewish roots. This disassociation of itself from its root became the stuff of the shadow.

In Charles Paterson's' book *Anti- Semites: The Road to the Holocaust and Beyond,* he shows the steady progression of Christians to separate from their Jewishness and to shift blame for the death of Jesus to the Jews and away from the Romans. All Jews themselves, Mark, Matthew, Paul, and even Luke and John, painted the Jews and Judaism as the forces that persecuted and drove Jesus to his death.

Early writings of the Church Fathers in the second, third, fourth, and fifth centuries - particularly those of John Chrysostom, a widely respected Doctor of the church and later made a saint - the shadow grew ever larger on the Jewish face. In his sermons he attacked the Jews of his city. He called them "lustful, rapacious, greedy, perfidious bandits, inveterate murderers, destroyers, men possessed by the devil." Their synagogue was a place of shame and ridicule. Jewish rites were criminal and impure. And why were the Jews so hateful? The answer said the Bishop, was in the gospels of the New Testament, which described how the Jews had killed Jesus.

In 1918 at the end of World WAR 1, Jung wrote, "That the animal in us becomes more beastlike when repressed". He cites the bloody wars of Christian nations and the slaughter of innocents, the repressed shadow of the Christian teachings being the culprit here. The Second World War advanced the repression and projected even more of the shadow onto the Jew.

The resentment felt by much of the Mideast, of Israel as a democratic, educated, successful nation, carved out of the desert, has continued to hold that nation as a container for more projections. Peace might finally be achieved when the less developed countries reclaim their lost birthrights of creativity, resourcefulness, personal freedom, and independence, thereby owning their shadows. This stays illusive. It's easier to wish Israel out of existence than to deal with becoming whole.

What then might be the shadow of Israel? Could it be the victim? To Israel the persona of warrior is a much more desirable one than victim of a holocaust. In *The Hero & His Shadow*, Israeli Jungian analyst Eril Shalit said "The conscious developments of warrior and aggressor have sent all signs of weakness and neediness to the shadow." Shalit observes:

> *The Palestinians have suffered considerably from this war. Like Israel and the Israelis are obliged to scrutinize their shadow, the Palestinians will need to withdraw their massive projections onto the enemy as the evil to be destroyed and to acknowledge guilt. (Shalit 1969)*

Successful minorities, both groups and individuals, provide easy scapegoats for the shadows of their members still struggling for success. The struggling minority often projects onto others the power of their positive unlived shadows, which include their native intelligence and independence, thereby resenting and even hating those in their own group and the majority who have succeeded.

We bestow Black athletes, musicians, and actors with much public acclaim and rightly so. Why then are the growing ranks of Black intellectual achievers, past and present, not given the same respect in the black community? Beginning as far back as the 18th century in America, there lived Benjamin Banneker, born in Maryland 1731. Banneker, a mostly self-educated man, invented among many other things the first functional clock that kept accurate time and ran for more than fifty years. There have been Black men and women PHDs, doctors, inventors, scientists, teachers, and successful people in business.

Perspective is everything. We decry the lack of diversity among CEOs in Fortune's 500 while more needs to be done to celebrate the successes. How many are aware of La June Montgomery at the helm of W. K. Kellogg Foundation as president and CEO, the first African–American to lead the foundation in its 83-year history. Another example would be Channing Dungey, 46, ABC's new entertainment president, which makes her the first African-American to head programming at a major broadcast network.

But neither the black nor the white communities, and especially not the government, stress or reward the many self-made, brilliant people who instead are often referred to as "Uncle Toms" or "acting white" by their own black communities.

I remember my own surprise that when Justice Clarence Thomas was made a Chief Justice and the black community did not celebrate his accomplishment. Instead, many turned against him.

The owning of the Shadow property of achievement, superiority, intelligence and independence in this community must first come from the community itself through acceptance and celebration of their high achievers in all walks of life while shirking the images of inferiority, victim, and dependency.

Blacks are not intellectually inferior; I believe a great number are intellectually repressed. A persistent collective belief of victimhood and inferiority will remain as long as their accomplishments in the world of the intellect are not given the attention they deserve. The black community itself led by its highest achievers must do the owning of the shadow.

Another group visible today in America are the baby boomers, which in the 1960s soundly turned their backs on anyone over thirty, hurtling this not to be trusted shadow on to the "evil and corrupt" big business, repressive parents, the government and any other holder that could contain the projection.

It is with fascination today when one sees them struggling as they are meeting up with their own "not to be trusted over 30" selves. Can they integrate maturity into their lives? Can they trust their aging selves? Some will, some will not.

And what of the shadow of the white majority United States? Certainly a history of genocidal treatment of Native Americans, enslavement of Afro-Americans, interment camps for Japanese and German citizens, bomb building, weapons selling, marginalization of many groups by color, nationality, race, sexual preference, gender and status, all became a part of our collective shadow. It becomes impossible to recognize true evil if we don't fully own our shadow.

While the distances between the Ghetto and the suburbs may be counted in miles, psychologically they are worlds apart and many a ghetto has become the perfect dumping ground for all we wish not to see about ourselves.

In the end it is not the shadow that is the villain in this story. Rather it is the ego of a person that decides who it wants to be, how it wants to appear to the world, what is good, what is bad, and in so doing throws away all that brings it into true relationship with its own Self. Our shadows are what give us our three dimensionality. The ego is the flat one-sidedness of us.

The evil we fear letting into our lives in the form of our shadows is never actually as capable of evildoing as our ego's acting out in the world without its shadow. One only has to look at the acts committed daily out of the ego's sense of righteousness to see the truth of this.

To many, the concept of owning our shadow is frightening. We are afraid that we will suddenly act out irresponsibly and even worse, destructively. But the truth is that by owning our shadow we become more conscious and more able to make choices in our behaviors instead of being the easy dupe for our dark side as well as that of the collective.

Poet Robert Bly, in *A Little Book On The Human Shadow,* speaks of the shadow as "the bag we all carry around on our backs, the bag that gets bigger and bigger the older we get, for it contains all that we re-press and deny about ourselves and about our lives."

Five

Persona

The Mask We Wear

Strategically, the mask is one of the best properties to own early. As the role we play in social situations it is closely connected to the ego. Jung named it the Persona. The word comes from the Greek word for the large masks that early Greek actors used to portray their characters. Have you ever enjoyed choosing and wearing a Halloween costume and for a brief and conscious moment becoming someone else?

I wonder what Jung would make of the world of cyberspace today where we may choose to create any avatar, a digital persona, and freely enter into virtual relationships on line with people all over the globe. It is nearly unbelievable that over two billion people worldwide have registered to play in the virtual World of War craft, Second life and Maple Story, often referred to as MMORP's (Massively Multiplayer

Online Role-Playing Game) In these games we can become the hero we have always dreamed of or the villain we can never express in life. This can be a fun, empowering experience and can be educational as long as we remain aware of our true selves and know why we chose the particular symbol.

The danger and the benefits lie in not removing the mask when the game is over. A person with low Self-esteem might emerge from a game with a better opinion of himself or herself, thereby benefiting. On the other hand, an already self-worshiping person might become more impossible to live with in daily life, after conquering worlds and people in the game.

Sometimes a mask is chosen for us, especially when we are young and eager to please. I remember a man I dated in my twenties who definitely knew what image he wanted me to project "hipper", "cooler" and more compliant than I ever really was. But when I finally stopped being who he wanted me to be, having become tired of play-acting, I shed the mask, returned to my less hip and cool self, and stood up to him. He promptly rejected me.

Most of us have a mask we wear to get along, although there are also those whose Mask is intended more for keeping people away. For the most part it is important and beneficial. We have the mask we wear at work, the mark of a true professional; the mask we wear with our friends, and the mask we wear with our families. There are many others. Teacher, student, celebrity, politician, helper, victim, gangster, happy masks, sad masks, survivor and on and on. All of the various masks we wear make up our Persona.

Owning this property means becoming conscious of our full wardrobe of masks and learning to separate them from our true selves. The masks themselves are seldom bad. They serve definite purposes in our lives. The danger lies in becoming so attached, and so identified with our favorite masks, that we are unable to tell where our Persona ends and we begin. We all know of the actor who becomes the part he plays or the mother who can't stop mothering, the boss who can't stop bossing, and the teacher who is always teaching. Jung said, "The result could be the shallow, brittle, conformist kind of personality which is 'all persona', with its excessive concern for what people think."

Our chosen professions have expected personas and as members we do our best to live up to the expectations. But if the time comes when we can no longer move easily between our various roles, our mask has become stuck to our faces. Consequently, we will severely limit any further self-knowledge. In effect we stop growing as persons. We have conveniently discarded the parts of our psyche we do not want to the property of our shadow and thereby have reduced the fullness of our lives.

There may not be a clear opportunity to own this property until the second half of life. If by this time our mask is glued to us, it is sure to be causing discomfort. Resentment grows as our true selves become more and more frustrated and angry at being forced to act in ways that are appropriate for the mask we are wearing but are now felt as empty, meaningless actions to the person living beneath the mask.

We know we are under the spell of the mask when we feel resentful, unsure of who we really are, inauthentic, phony, and tired of pleasing other people or perhaps even of fooling others. The mask we have put on serves several purposes; to make a favorable impression; to keep us from being too vulnerable in unfamiliar situations; to conceal our inner Self from prying eyes, and sometimes to deliberately create a false impression in order to manipulate an outcome. Celebrity Bill Cosby, former Christian Television pioneer Jim Baker, and O.J. Simpson are just a few that come to mind who wore their moral, hero good guy masks while practicing outrageous, scandalous behavior. When their true selves were revealed we could hardly believe it. And particularly sad was beloved Robin Williams who made us all laugh and whose comic, happy mask hid his deep pain. These men may never have descended to such depths if their permanent masks were not so grandiose. Whatever the reason, we find ourselves acting in ways that are contrary to our true selves and the conflict and tension often become unbearable.

This is the start of many a midlife crisis or as I prefer to think of it, as a midlife gift. For if we own our mask at this time we may be able to separate from it and free ourselves to become more of who we really are and to accelerate our progress in building our inner estates.

If instead we choose not to own the mask property, we may well be doomed to a dangerous war with ourselves. In Archetypes and the Collective Unconscious Jung said "We yield too much to the ridiculous fear that we are at bottom quite impossible beings, that if everyone were to appear as he really is a frightful social catastrophe would ensue."

For the most part masks are essential in an orderly society and beneficial to us in many ways. What is crucial is that we are conscious enough to take them off and put them on when we need to, staying always aware of whom we really are and why we are choosing a particular mask.

Six

Personality Types

One of the great assets we human beings possess, our differences, are frequently overlooked as being valuable. Instead they are blamed for our misunderstanding and broken relationships.

It is true, personality differences are always present in these failed situations, but the real culprit is our failure to see them as the gifts they are, and our learned attitudes of fear, hatred, and rejection toward them. When properly seen as gifts, it is our differences that shed the needed light on our misunderstandings and mend our broken relationships.

At first awareness we may only learn to tolerate the differences; next we can move on to gain understanding and acceptance, and finally, we might actually come to love and welcome them. Each encounter will lead us further and deeper toward wholeness.

Jung and Freud, for many years had a close relationship built on their common interests and collaboration in psychoanalysis. Jung looked up to Freud as a father figure and had great respect for him, and Freud referred to Jung as "my friend, my helper, and my heir." But there was at the same time always a difference between their personalities that acted like a grain of sand in the oyster, irritating, yet at the same time a potential jewel. Finally the dogmatic, sexuality-based approach of Freud and the scientific and spiritual approach of Jung collided head on and their differences in the end separated them forever.

In the next years as Jung reflected on what had happened, the grain of sand become the pearl, as he gave birth to his study of personality types, which gave us words such as extrovert and introvert and so much more. Jung knew there was something so fundamentally different between himself and Freud; it had to be more than disagreement over theory or professional jealousy. It was more a different way of being that was as foreign to the other as if they had been from two different planets. For each type does indeed speak its own language. In a letter to Freud, Jung said:

> *Our personal differences will make our work different. You dig up the precious stones, but I have the degree of extension...and because of the difference in our working methods we shall undoubtedly meet from time to time in unexpected places. (Jung 1988)*

What Jung learned for himself and for each of us, was what appeared different and unpleasant to him about Freud was the forgotten and undeveloped side of his own personality. It was a side he disliked and mostly did not recognize and therefore had no use or respect for. This awareness became the catalyst for his work on personality types. As Jung explained, "Everything that irritates us about others can lead us to an understanding of ourselves."

He theorized we are born with a particular attitude that is natural to us and usually can be seen in a child as early as one-year old and that can be further intensified through our environment. This attitude is either extroverted or introverted, words he introduced in his classic text, Psychological Types, and changes little during our lifetime.

As we progress through life we find in addition to this basic attitude, we also have a natural way of reacting and adapting to the people and events we encounter which is most comfortable for us and done without real effort. As Jung himself said "Our main outlines are already laid down in our psyches."

At the same time, there are ways of being, which are not at all natural and which we tend to avoid at all cost. If we try to act out in these alien ways, we are uncomfortable and definitely feel like the proverbial fish out of water.

These preferences for what is comfortable soon shape our personalities. Jung found four such types of personalities. He called them functions of consciousness and named them thinking, feeling, intuition, and sensation. Thinking and its opposite, feeling are one pair and Intuition and its opposite, sensation, are the second pair.

Intuition	Thinking
Sensation	Feeling

Sensation tells us what a thing is through our five senses, thinking tells us what it is factually. Feeling tells us what this thing means to us and Intuition tells us what is the potential of a thing for us.

Jung found while each of us has one personality type that is superior to the others, we also have a second type that is easily accessible to us. This second one will always belong to the adjoining pair. If you are an intuitive type your secondary functions are either thinking or feeling, but never the direct opposite, sensation. This least available type, Jung called inferior. Feeling is always opposite of thinking and sensation is always the opposite of intuition. As Jung notes:

We should not pretend to understand the world only by the intellect; we apprehend it just as much by feeling. Therefore, the judgment of the intellect is, at best, only half of truth, and must, if it be honest, also come to an understanding of its inadequacy. (Jung 1928)

It is this inferior side we have so much trouble recognizing in ourselves and dislike intensely when we see it in others. We are perfectly able to go through life without using our inferior function and so we do.

In fact, society needs and almost demands our superior function. According to Jung it was around the time of Christ that we began to live in a collective culture, and this collective atmosphere proved detrimental to the individual development. Jung wrote:

The privileged position of the superior function is as detrimental to the individual as it is valuable to the society. It is not man who counts, but his one differentiated (superior) function. (Jung 1921)

Man no longer appears as man in our culture; he is represented by a function. What is more, he identifies completely with this function and denies the relevance of the other inferior functions... beneath the neglected functions are individual values which, while of small importance for collective life, are of the greatest value for individual life.

> *While our superior function gets us what we need from our collective existence it does not offer us the satisfaction and the joie de vivre, which we get from the development of our individual values...,Our true selves are much more contained within our inferior function, which lives in the unconscious. To find our true individuality it is here we must journey.* (Jung 1921)

It only takes meeting a person whose superior function is our inferior one to see the implications. While the study of type helps in knowing ourselves it does a larger service in providing an understanding and acceptance of the others in our lives and in our world. In other words, it enables us to develop an awareness that we all are different in our approach to life and that this is okay.

In the case of Jung and Freud, Jung was an introverted, thinking, intuitive type and Freud probably an extroverted, sensation, feeling type. This could certainly have accounted for both their attraction and eventual falling out.

In the beginning of a relationship we often find that rather than being repelled by our opposite function, we may be strongly attracted. Jung observed many marriages are based on this attraction of opposites. For in this way an introvert can marry an extrovert and can for a time feel relieved of having to try to be what is so distasteful for him or her. A "thinking" type can think for the family and a "feeling" type can do the feeling.

Our hope is the other will do for us the things we cannot and do not want to do. But this better half arrangement seldom lasts a lifetime. The time comes when the "other" refuses to carry the load all alone; or we become so terribly bored with ourselves and as von Franz says, "Our superior function is worn out - begins to rattle and lose oil like an old car."

Jung describes the absence of our inferior function "as a painful wound and this accounts greatly for the feeling that something is missing, so common to our midlife."

We may also stop feeling the attraction we once did for the opposite and only feel the dis-attraction. The introvert may become tired of an extroverted mate who constantly brings the world into his or her private space.

When the time comes for us to own the property of the inferior function, we often do so screaming and kicking, and yet it is this alone that "holds the secret key" to our wholeness. Von Franz writes, "...if people succeed in turning to their inferior function, they will rediscover a new potential of life."

In *Psychological Types* Joseph Wheelwright, tells of a dream Jung had after his breakup with Freud, which pointed out to Jung clearly that he was indeed a thinking type and if his feeling were to come up, he would have to sacrifice his thinking. He did not mean "he was going to murder it for ever and ever, but it did mean it had to be temporarily out of business in order to allow the feeling function to emerge." This is not an easy or attractive prospect to someone who does not value the feeling side, but it is a heroic act.

In determining our attitude, it is not hard to spot the extrovert. This person is often talkative, able to relate easily to many people, even at the same time. As a property the extrovert is right out in the open, top of the hill, on a main street, clearly visible. An extrovert moves energetically through life toward the objects in his view. His energy (libido) flows outward toward the object, be it work, people, events or things - the reclusive life is not for him. He prefers groups and needs the objective world to be the container for his energies.

The introverted person, on the other hand, lives more in the background. As a property this one is definitely off the beaten path. Rather than the energy flowing out of his psyche he is pulling it subjectively into himself from the world. This can be overwhelming and so he has the need to control how much he lets in. The unknown can be fearful, and reclusiveness is often a welcome respite from the world. Introverts do not easily reveal themselves to others. They are in better relationship to ideas than things.

At the end of life the extrovert may be in for quite a shock when realizing what his less expressive counterpart actually accomplished in a lifetime.

While we have an attitude, which may be extroverted or introverted, our unconscious also has an attitude, which is repressed and is the opposite of our conscious attitude. There can come a time when the extrovert deeply craves the more inner life of the introvert and vice versa.

In America, introverts are outnumbered about three to one. As a result they must develop extra coping skills early in life because there will be an inordinate amount of pressure on them to "shape up", to act like the rest of the world. The introvert is pressured daily, almost from the moment of awakening to respond and conform to the outer world.

Whether introverted or extroverted in style, differences grow even wider when function is added to style. So an introverted thinking type and an introverted feeling type will not approach life in the same way and consequently will not have much understanding of the other's style even though both are introverted. Just as an extroverted intuitive bounces merrily through life from one adventure to another an extroverted sensation is much more comfortable to stay in the here and now.

We are all born with access to each type and function. But we go through life relying on our superior ones, which works very well in the first half of our lives, but eventually limits our potential for becoming whole. True excitement and renewal comes when we finally turn to our inferior type and function, and develop these properties. This is what brings us to understand the other and to our reunion with our true self.

Seven

Which One Are You?

*"One becomes two
Two becomes three,
And out of the third comes the one as the fourth."
(Alchemist riddle)*

Over my many years in the Real Estate business I
believe I have encountered every type of
personality that exists. As a matter of fact it was of
great help to me professionally to become aware of
the various attitudes and functions described by Jung,
for my approach to the buyers and sellers could be
adjusted accordingly. Nothing can put off an
introverted buyer more than an overly aggressive,
extroverted sales person. More importantly the
decision-making process is greatly affected by the
personality type.

I can always do a better job for my buyer or seller or even the other agent involved, if I attempt to gain understanding of their superior type. While it sounds complicated there are many signals.

An extroverted-thinking person gathers a mass of data. They read books on real estate and all relevant news articles. These are the clients who actually read the contract (not every one does.) Their energies flow into the outer situation in order to fit in the facts they have gathered. Their actions are mostly a result of their analysis of the facts they have accumulated.

In negotiations, this buyer is not likely to be receptive to an emotional appeal. The intellect reigns. They know all the rules and if a problem arises they are first with an answer. Sometimes in the sale of a home there needs to be a bending of the rule, a little give. This type of buyer is least likely to be able to do this. The danger of the extroverted-thinking person is in becoming too rigid. They can become petty and even hostile to those who do not go along with their meticulous plan. They often gain their point but in the process lose the home.

The introverted thinker is not as able as his extroverted counterpart to express himself or herself verbally and the facts they gather are more for the purpose of verifying their inner images. This type searches for clarity and order relating to their images of how things should be rather than to the facts existing in the outer world.

As a buyer they have inner clarity regarding the home they want to buy, the difficulty comes in linking to the reality of what they can buy. This thinking style can become overly complicated and careful. Only with the greatest difficulty can this person admit what is clear to him may not be equally clear to everyone else.

As a realtor I have a difficult time reading the needs of the introverted-thinking person. I have to do a lot of guessing as to what they really want and more explaining of what is actually possible. It takes much tact to deal with this type for any hint of criticism of their ideas can turn them cold and cause them to withdraw.

Like a master chess player this client gets involved with every detail and every aspect of their theory, and the game is everything. While they have studied all there is to know about real estate, their concern with the rules and strategies often take precedence over actually consummating a transaction. I never expect a quick sale with an introverted-thinking client.

Some have postulated Jung was this type and while his contribution is invaluable, much of his writing is hard to grasp because of the volume and complexity of it alone. It had to be interpreted by many more extroverted and/or feeling types to be available to a more general audience.

The extroverted-feeling person is definite about what they like and dislike. This type is also known as the judging type. As they walk through a property they feel it. This person may want to leave after walking through the front door due to a negative feeling, or want to buy it when standing on the curb. They freely speak the feelings that flit across their minds as they come, forming quick opinions of the home, the owners, the neighbors, etc. They also can easily change their minds once the first rush of feeling leaves them. Out of their changeability they can be moody and turn on even their closest associates.

However, the extroverted-feeling person is the person who will uphold the traditional values of the society. They do not like those who don't. When extroverted, they will often be in the helping professions. It is to this type society owes thanks for maintaining traditional social standards. Jung said, "The function is designed not to upset the general feeling situation." While this type wants to win, they are the ones who do not enjoy doing it at the expense of another. They care that the seller is not hurt by the sale. They do not feel "right" causing someone else to lose.

Jung points out that fashions owe their existence to the extroverted feeling type and the whole positive support of social, philanthropic, and cultural enterprises. Without extroverted feeling, a harmonious social life would be impossible." But if this type gets too one-sided or exaggerated they can become "cold", "unfeeling" and "untrustworthy." They are capable of hurting the feelings of others in a vicious way.

The introverted feeling person is more inaccessible and silent. Still waters run deep may be said of this type. The introverted feeling person is intense and hard to read since their inner motives remain hidden. They do not have to say anything and generally will not, but this type exerts a secret yet positive influence on their surroundings by setting standards. They often form the ethical backbone of a group or negatively can be sensed as a "domineering influence, often difficult to define.... a sort of stifling or oppressive feeling which holds everybody...under a spell", as Jung describes. I know I'm dealing with this type when I sense myself being judged without any words spoken. This buyer keeps me aware throughout the process of my actions and myself as I feel their silent judgments.

They can benefit by finding artistic expression for their intense inner feelings. Therapy for the introverted feeling type can be useful.

The extroverted intuitive type relies on a kind of inner knowing which they cannot explain. They seem to know what is going to happen before anyone else and can amaze us by plucking answers from the air. In the real estate transaction they have a good feel for what the outcome will be. They are good negotiators because they have an innate understanding of what will make the deal happen. Their hunches are often right.

This type is not much aware of their physical being or surroundings. In shopping for a home they are seldom aware of the details of the house, the colors, textures etc. It's the house as a whole they get, not the parts. These folks are tireless in their search, forgetting to stop for rest or refreshment.

They see the potential in every home. 'What if we knock out this wall, add on here and move this', is their common approach to looking. They are always thinking 'what if...' and answering themselves from their hunch about a thing. They live in a world of possibilities. They are often the innovators in the world of business and able to know what the people want and what will be popular next year.

These are the people who hold the knife to the cutting edge. Their downfall comes from the fact they are easily bored and often waste their talents by jumping around from project to project.

The introverted intuitive seems to be the gatekeeper to all the properties in the unconscious since the inner world is familiar ground to this person. This does not mean they do not have their work to do, but they will not feel as alien in the inner world as other types might. In fact, this is the person who often helps others as therapist or analyst to bridge the barriers to their own inferior functions.

Many introverted intuitives are to be found among artists and poets, for they are able through their creations to communicate that which lies deep within the unconscious. According to Jung this type could also be a seer or a crank. Often out of touch with their bodies they have great difficulty in noticing the needs of the body and in controlling its appetites. They often suffer from hypochondria and compulsive behaviors.

As a buyer the introverted intuitive leaps around in their search for a home, seemingly without a system. They do not prefer the straight line at all. Always searching out the new before they have finished with the old, it is hard to get them to choose an area, a kind of house, etc. since they are seeing other possibilities. The danger to them comes if they never develop their inferior opposite sensation function. For while they see the potential in the outer world of people and things, they often neglect their own development and for this reason can be much helped by touching their opposite inferior sensation, which can act as a kite string to their urge to fly through life.

The sensation type on the other hand is purely involved with their bodies, their environment, and the physical material aspects of their lives. They love the physicality of life with the many colors, textures, and beauties. They observe the world and the people in it carefully, taking pleasure in noting the details. When I show houses to this type, they show me the home, because as an intuitive person myself I miss much of what they always see. They see and appreciate the textures of a tile, the color of a wall, the individual plants in the garden. They know if I haven't washed my car or if I've changed my hair or makeup. They notice the clothes we wear and the food we eat. They live in the moment; they seldom look ahead or behind but at any time can give a clear physical description of where they are.

If extroverted sensation, Jung says, no other human type can equal them in realism. They accumulate experiences and material objects like the thinker gathers facts yet they are not able to put these experiences to use without eventually developing their inferior opposite, intuition. Their aim is the enjoyment of each experience and the sensation they receive from it. They are not introspective and in the negative can be crudely sensual.

As clients they are likely to move least often since they are grounded in each moment and do not see much sense in looking elsewhere. But if they become too one-sided, they can get lost in the world of their senses. If they break the one-sidedness and begin their journey to their opposite, intuition, they can bring new depth and meaning to their experiences.

The introverted sensation type is a different person and being unable to express themselves outwardly, they tend to turn to art and abstractions. They can appear calm and passive, and may be frequently misjudged as stupid, but this is because they are slow to relate their quick inner processes to the outer world and so they appear to be not connected to it at all.

They go through life with only their senses directing them and while they cannot verbalize well what they experience, they can produce an inner image of it easily. In painting a landscape, only the artist may recognize the tree he produces, for it has lost its objective qualities and has been reproduced in the way this type senses it. A great deal of impressionist art and certainly abstract art of all kinds requires a well-developed introverted sensation function. An example of how misunderstandings occur is to watch an extroverted thinking type trying to make the introverted sensation person's tree into a "real" one.

I have had a few introverted sensation clients of this type over the years and because this is so opposite to my type I find it hard to understand them. As buyers they are least likely to buy a home for any practical reason and while their choices can be mistaken as irrational, I know they are in their comfort zone.

They often live in a world of illusion and mysticism. Introverted sensation sees and understands the background of the outer world rather than its surface. They grasp what went before them and what will come after their passing but they are not much in touch with the objective outer world. Their senses reach into the past and the present while the extroverted sensation seizes on the momentary existence of things they can see.

Joining Forces

These foregoing functions exist in each of us and even though we make use of the easily accessible and more conscious ones through most of our lives, we can exhibit a mixture and it may be hard to identify our own preferences. The easiest way to find our superior type is to find our inferior one first.

Franz says, "The inferior function is the door through which all the figures of the unconscious come into consciousness."(von Franz 1961). She compares our consciousness to a room with four doors and it is the fourth door through which all the major properties in the unconscious can break into consciousness. She explains, "Because the inferior function...is naturally the weak spot... these unconscious parts of us can break in here."

Your fourth door can be recognized as your "touchy" spot. If you are devastated when your thinking is criticized you can be sure this is your weak area; if you cannot bear to have your judgments questioned, feeling is your fourth door; if you are vulnerable when your view of reality or your sensory impressions are attacked, sensation is probably your nemesis; and inferior intuition cannot stand to have its guesses or more accurately their suspicions challenged.

The sensation types can find themselves longing for more than the day at a time view they have of life. They're tired of being the ground and the anchor for their more adventurous friends and they may need greater and greater sensations in order to feel satisfied. They easily may be suffering physically (Briggs) from leading an excessive or compulsive sensual existence. They may want to extract greater meaning from their experiences.

At this time it is crucial to be aware of what is going on so we do not feel completely deserted by our trusted old friend, our superior function. It is merely a transitional stage on the way to rediscovering the world in a whole new way. There is no way to open the fourth door without feeling as though the whole building will collapse.

What is to be done? Are we doomed to lose what we identify as the best side of ourselves? Not at all. But neither can we just flip to the other side. Like life itself, it is a process and it involves sacrifice, courage, and faith.

First we must temporarily sacrifice the comfortable successful, superior function, which feels like all we are and decide consciously not to use this function for a while. It is the same as a right-handed person tying that arm behind his back for just awhile, long enough to experience the left hand and what it is capable of.

To reach our most inferior function we must move down to where it lives in the unconscious but we must descend slowly, with awareness, using our other functions as stepping-stones.

We cannot suddenly decide to go from thinking to its opposite, which is feeling, or from intuition to its opposite sensation. We must work through a long and slow process, living with each newly discovered function one at a time as a main one.

If our superior type is thinking we must first go to our intuition or sensation, whichever is closest to us and then to its opposite. Only after we have these three consciously available can we even touch the fourth, our inferior feeling function.

It will be left to the reader to pursue the many avenues available for a further study of personality type. A good resource for further study is the Myers-Briggs Type Indicator, (MBTI) test. An online test is available as well as those administered by professionals. The book Please Understand me by David Keirsey and Marilyn Bates is also enlightening on this subject.

In my own life, my type is intuitive, feeling. Midlife for me brought much discontent. While I was successful in business and in my relationships, I felt something missing in myself. I lived as a pebble skipping over the water of my life, not at all sure where I would land. Life was speeding by and I had not fulfilled any of my deepest longings, which later turned out to be a reconnection with my Self and the whole person I was truly meant to be. I fortunately had my experiences in Jungian thought to help me realize I desperately needed to touch my inferior functions.

To accomplish this I needed to slow down in my chase of the potential in all things and people. My second available function of feeling had served me well in my relationships and added stability to my life but I had to turn to thinking which was not readily available to me and this meant I needed to practice new ways of being.

First I consciously attempted to go deeper into those things that were of interest to me. I made the effort to study in more than the superficial way I had done all my life. I had always been a "jack-of-all-trades master of none."

I consciously changed this by focusing my attention on one thing. I picked painting as a way to focus and while I began to study art in a deeper way, forcing me to think, I was able to touch for the first time the sensation function, which had eluded me throughout my life. After much time spent in deeper study of the subject I became more able to pick up thinking when I needed it. Now thinking is no longer foreign to me. The most elusive function remaining for me to own is Sensation and I am still not fully intimate with it but it is no longer foreign.

I was attending a funeral and had dressed with as much care as is usual for me, which was not much. I was deep in conversation with a beautiful, extremely well groomed, young French woman with an obvious high degree of developed sensation. She leaned over and whispered in my ear confidentially, "Do you know you have two different colored socks on?" Horrified I looked down and sure enough under my slacks I saw one blue and one black. I laughed and was embarrassed, but not surprised.

In order to touch this fourth function in myself I had to put a hold on my superior functions for a while. My usual way of flying through life had caused me to miss many of the amazing details that are visible only to the well-developed sensation types. This means involving the senses. It means tasting my food, not just eating it, hearing the wind and the water, feeling the texture of my clothes against my body, noticing the details of daily life, what time the sun rises and sets, the temperature of the day, whether I am hot or cold? Believe it or not, as an intuitive I can miss all of this.

I experienced an amazing awakening by having the opportunity to visit Japan several times, a country whose sensation function is everywhere alive. Purchasing a loaf of bread wrapped with care and tied with a bow, eating with chopsticks so that I actually tasted my food, even the hardware store was an aesthetic wonder. I spent hours in my favorite stationery store, just soaking in the incredible selections of colorful papers, many handmade, pens I'd never seen before, and notebooks of every size and description.

All artfully displayed. And the most awesome thing happened. After spending quite a bit of time in this sensation-laden country I felt a strange and new at-homeness. I felt complete. It was as if I came home to my self. My entire aesthetic life changed after that. A lost part of me was restored and is with me to this day.

I can easily lose touch with my fourth function but I have become conscious enough to know when I am living a lopsided existence. At these times I can go to my sensation function as a helper that will bring me back into balance, and no, we never lose our superior function. Instead we become whole and gain allies for life.

Norman Cousins in his book Anatomy of An Illness, described his use of laughter to heal himself of a serious illness. In reading his work and hearing him speak my impression of Cousins was that of a serious, rational, highly developed, thinking type of person. One can see that through a willingness to sacrifice his rational, thinking side and suspend disbelief for a while, he was able to go down to where his feelings and senses waited, where he could laugh, perhaps until he cried, and lubricate himself with feeling.

He healed himself of that illness and while laughter was his principal medicine, for someone else the prescription might be different. In the beginning stages of his illness, he felt "wrung out", a common feeling for the dryness of thinking. Cousins describes how he began his pursuit of feeling in a typically thinking way. "A plan began to form in my mind for systematic pursuit of the salutary emotions."

He proceeded to use his thinking to amass the facts he needed regarding his illness and then definitely became an expert in his own right. But then in an intuitive leap, he began to enter the world of the senses. To improve his environment and his nutrition - his material world - he moved out of the hospital into a hotel room. He had already begun his now legendary viewing of funny movies and this continued in his hotel. He gained many pain-free moments following bouts of belly laughing. In summing up his healing Cousins said, "Though I can't be sure of this point I have a hunch (intuition) that my own total involvement was a major factor in my recovery."

I suggest the total involvement he spoke of was an involvement of a side of himself that had been left behind in the development and preference of his brilliant thinking and intuition. While Cousins did not in anyway lose his superior thinking function, I think he found and brought out of the darkness, his inferior functions of feeling and sensation and thereby regained a "healthy" balance.

It is important to say this does not imply Cousins had no feelings. Of course he did. Often, we may overcompensate for an inferior function with extraordinary acts as may be seen in the remarkable good works for peace Cousins performed. Because a function is inferior does not mean it doesn't exist, but only that we cannot call it up easily or naturally and we will be slow in this area. A thinking person can think about their feelings but cannot always feel them. Just as a feeling person cannot know what they think as readily as they know what they feel.

Cousins wrote, "Studies show that up to 90% of patients who reach out for medical help are suffering from self-limiting disorders well within the range of the body's own healing powers." I propose this limitation of the Self is what each of us must deal with in our own unique way.

For a feeling type, "healing" may more likely come from learning, perhaps for the first time in their life what they think, by suspending temporarily the values of the society at large and begin to think their own thoughts. Cousins provided us with an inspiring picture of a thinker who suspended thinking long enough to feel his joy and laughter. The intuitive can discover the pleasure and beauty of the material world and the wonder of the miraculous details of life. And sensation can enter the world of ideas and possibilities, gaining new hope and vision.

And out of the Third comes the Fourth

This line from an alchemist riddle that started this chapter is the appropriate finish. For when we have moved through the three functions into the fourth and have owned it, then "comes the one." This is a completely new function that Jung called the transcendent function. Von Franz describes it best:

> *When someone has gone through this transformation he can use his thinking function, if that is the appropriate reaction, or he can let intuition or sensation come into operation, but he is no longer possessed by one dominant function. The ego can take up a particular function and put it down, like a tool, in an awareness of its own reality outside the system of the four functions...the inferior function is an important bridge to the experience of the deeper layers of the unconscious, going to it and staying with it, not just taking a quick bath in it, effects a tremendous change in the whole structure of the personality. (von Franz 2001)*

Consciously reaching the transcendent function can make us an undisputed master of our lives. In reality, simply becoming conscious of the inferior function and accepting it as a part of us will initiate a union of these opposites.

By gaining the awareness that we originally dumped our inferior functions into the unconscious because they represented a threat to our goals in life, we also come to see that ultimately this one-sidedness will keep us from individuation. For the pursuit of our one-sided interests is not the way to individuation, which is concerned more with the perfecting of human individuality. Jung says "The conscious acceptance of repressed functions is equivalent to an internal civil war; the opposites previously restrained, are unleashed."

A person entering into the process of owning their inferior and neglected property is worthy in their own right and will reap the reward of infinite growth and maturity and perhaps for the benefit of mankind, we will at least learn to tolerate and maybe eventually love the differences.

Eight

Battle of the Sexes

Masculine, Feminine, Male, Female, Woman, Man. Today in American culture much discussion swirls around the definitions of these words. Is there a difference between the sexes? Can men do what women do and vice versa? Is there equal pay and equal opportunity? We deal with same sex partners, Lesbian, Gay, bisexual and transgender rights and defining these has given rise to gender studies in our universities. All of these curricula focus on the intersection of gender with race, ethnicity, class, nationality, or disability. Also, there are further classifications within the communities of LGBTQ, which stand for Lesbian, Gay, Bisexual, Transgender, and Queer, or Questioning.

However the battle of the sexes discussed in this book is not the one studied in the above-mentioned courses. The battle here does not take place in the global, societal, or cultural environment but is much more a personal civil war, played out within our own psyches, with our own biology and guided by Jung's work. He found initially within his psyche and later through his work with clients (analysands) and mental patients, that within each male there lives an unconscious female component he called the Anima which corresponds to a man's soul. Within each female, there exists a male component that he called Animus, which corresponds to a woman's spirit. These contra-sexual partners, I will call properties. Jung called them archetypes. They are called the invisible partners in John Sander's classic work by that same name. Whether we were born male or female or LGBTQ we are all born as androgynous beings and these anima and animus energies, when repressed, will make unexpected appearances in our lives in some form or other. Therefore, this battle is personal and unique to each human being.

Does this battle affect the larger society? Of course. Our relationship to these inner properties influences our interaction with our male and female contacts as well as our personal identities. Mother son, father daughter, sister brother, boyfriend girlfriend, husband wife, employers employees. But ultimately each person must undertake the journey to his or her inner world alone.

The first appearance of these figures in our psyche is between father and daughter and mother and son. In the case of absent fathers and mothers, any father or mother figures that have a close relationship to the child will affect its psyche early on. This initiates what Jung called the first stage of development of these properties and lays the groundwork for our future relationships with the opposite sex.

Sisters and brothers often taste of the conflict that occurs as these Anima/Animus properties gain strength in our unconscious. And boys and girls go through school together for many years manning their battle stations, oblivious to the confusion they are experiencing.

First love brings new and even more confusing aspects of a person's outward battle for now hate and love, agony and pleasure, rejection and acceptance, become mixed together and we soon become aware that relating to the opposite sex is far from the easy matter portrayed in romantic movies, books and "happily ever after" stories of all kinds. The reason of course is that these fictional stories can never replicate the actual experiences and feelings that tear at a person who has fallen in love.

We proceed through the first half of life then, fighting these outer gender battles the best we can, licking our wounds, picking ourselves up, determined not to repeat our mistakes and finally, battle wearied and wounded, we may begin to get an inkling that the problem is not out there in the world of the opposite sex after all, but it is inside of us. In time we notice that unruly feelings seem to come from within and often go out of our control, causing us to repeatedly end up disenchanted. Finally when self-awareness dawns upon us we are ready to own the properties which Jung named the Anima and Animus.

These properties, like the Shadow, create a bridge from our conscious minds to the deepest part of our psyches. But until our ego is willing to acknowledge that, by itself, it does not have all the answers and instead becomes willing to begin the inward search, the Anima and the Animus can and will get us into trouble and cause untold suffering.

You meet your "soul" mate. It's love almost at first sight. You feel alive. This is the one. Really? Or have our soul qualities of Anima and Animus found each other? Have we fallen in love with an unlived and unrecognized part of ourselves? This is Projection. In real estate terms, it is like an encroachment of you upon another's property. For a while we project onto the other our inner image of our ideal or sometimes destructive invisible partner. This leads to unrealistic expectations, which the other can never live up to.

The Anima and the Animus are, as John Sanford called them, the Invisible Partners in every human relationship and in every person's search for individual wholeness. And what happens when the projection of the Anima property onto the love object fades as real life and the real person begin to appear? If we remain unconscious of this property we may languish in an early stage of development, incapable of lasting relationships, since out of disappointment with the "real person" the other has become, we move on to find a new subject to project upon.

Change can only happen through finally choosing to own and acknowledge this property and accepting responsibility for the grief it is causing. This choice gives us a chance to stay the course rather than fleeing and moving on.

If these inner partners are unable to find free expression and a home in our consciousness, they may turn to their dark side and lose themselves in sensuousness and materialism. They may exhibit a high degree of insensitivity, becoming domineering, possessive, and destructive to all the creative gifts and things of the spirit. Many a man and woman have become locked into the dark side of these archetypes and freeing them has everything to do with fully owning and developing them.

The stages of development

Jung noted the Anima and the Animus develop in four stages during our lifetime and while we are "possessed" by them, they will compel us to either overvalue or protest against the outer men and women in our lives, depending on what images of the other we have developed. "Possession," according to Jung "denotes a peculiar state of mind characterized by the fact that certain psychic contents, the so-called complexes, take over the control of the total personality in place of the ego, at least temporarily, to such a degree that the free will of the ego is suspended." A woman possessed by the Animus is always in danger of losing her femininity.

Jung personified the four stages of the development of the Anima. For a man the first stage is Eve, the mother, images of which are formed from his own mother either positive or negative. If he remains unconscious of this Anima figure he may always seek out women who will mother him, for better or for worse and never come into his own manhood.

In a man's second stage Jung personified Helen of Troy, who in Greek mythology was the most beautiful woman in the world and was accepted as the ideal of beauty. She is much connected to a man's sexual side of life. These second stage images can range from idealized woman to whore. A friend of mine once wrote of a whore with a soul spotted white, an image I never forgot since I thought it represented his Anima. He searched for women who were sexually loose but with virginal qualities. Hard to find.

In the third stage, the Anima is now raised to a man's spiritual development, personified in Mary, the mother of Jesus.

The fourth stage is symbolized by Jung as Sophia, an honored Goddess of Wisdom and the carrier of the man's wisdom.

The latter two stages are typically not gained until after midlife and become a worthy goal for a man at this time of life. However, it is fully possible that a man can languish in an early stage of development his whole life. An example may be a man who marries his "mother" and becomes so comfortable with being mothered and taken care of emotionally, he never fully develops as a man. Or the man who forever seeks his idealized woman of stage two and spends a lifetime moving from one relationship to another each time the "real woman" emerges and can no longer act as a suitable container for his projected ideal woman.

For the stages of growth of a woman's Animus, I have chosen to include the description of Jung's close associate, von Franz, because, as a woman, she possessed the added element of her personal experience.

> *In real life, it takes a long time for a woman to bring the Animus into consciousness, and it costs her a great deal of suffering. But if she succeeds in freeing herself from the Animus possession, he changes into an "inner companion of the highest value, who confers on her*

*positive masculine qualities such as initiative, courage,
objectivity, and intellectual clarity. (von Franz 1997)*

Like the Anima in a man, the Animus also commonly exhibits itself in four stages of development in women. "In the first stage he manifests as a symbol of physical force, for example, a sports hero." Jung added a thug and a man of power as images that may appear in her dreams and fantasies.

Her real-life father shapes a large part of this first stage of development of her inner man. The positive images we hold of the father are "protective, strengthening and reassuring, offering a woman a sense of security in the world. Jung said. The developing woman who remains unaware of this part of herself and becomes possessed by it, repeatedly will project her own inner father onto men who play father to her, taking care of her, patronizing her and expecting her to obey. Thus she gets to stay in a state of constant girlhood.

If, instead, the father was in fact abusive, controlling, and lacking in assurances, the woman will find herself insecure and drawn to men who are not threatening, but rather can be controlled by her in her attempts to feel safe. Only when she owns this property and uses her own strength and protective ways will she be free of her need for weak men. If she acknowledges her own part in keeping the man weak, she gifts him an opportunity to grow into his manhood and their relationship can prosper.

The strong, virile man symbolizes the second stage of development of the woman's Animus an athlete, romantic figures, a fixit-man, Harrison Ford, James Bond, or even the Terminator are types of images that may appear in her dreams and fantasies and represent her strength and independence. This is the time for her to seek adventure and take initiative. Women in their unawareness may find themselves attracted to the negative aspects of this stage restless, adventure-seeking kinds of partners. If so, the ability to sustain lasting relationships continues to elude them.

In the third stage, the Animus becomes "the word" and is therefore frequently projected onto noteworthy intellectuals, like clergy, professors, and spiritual guides of all kind. In this third stage a woman begins to rise into the spiritual realm and to start to feel within herself the stirrings of questions of meaning. This generally happens at the start of midlife. Also at this time Jung adds, "Woman can now relate to a man not only as husband but a lover and individual in his own right."

Von Franz continues, "On the fourth level, the Animus embodies the mind and becomes a mediator of creative and religious inner experiences, through which life acquires an individual meaning."

Jung says, "Finally, in his fourth manifestation, the Animus is the incarnation of meaning."As von Franz explains:

> At this stage he confers on a woman a spiritual and in-
> tellectual solidity that counterbalances her essentially
> soft nature. He can then act as a liaison connecting her
> with the spiritual life of the time. The creative courage
> in the truth conferred by the Animus gives a woman
> the daring to enunciate new ideas that can inspire oth-
> ers.

> The nature of woman is more closely related to the irra-
> tional, and this makes a woman better able to open to
> new inspirations from the unconscious. The very fact
> that women normally participate less in public life
> than men do makes it possible for their Animus to act
> as a "hidden prince" in the darkness of private life and
> bring about beneficial results. (von Franz 1997)

I think of First Ladies Nancy Reagan and Eleanor Roosevelt, whose positive Animus development was an asset to their President husbands. The last stage of development is not reached often in modern times but is most needed of all if we are to survive as a species. It is the Wise (often old) man residing in a woman. Apt symbols for this stage are Moses, Solomon, and Hermes, the messenger of the Gods. These wise inner properties bring "creativity, wisdom, vision, spiritual insight, and a bridge to the mind of God."

And what of the woman who does not own this fourth stage? She gives up her own creativity, vision, and spiritual insight and allows the real man in her life or others to act as her gurus and all-seeing prophets. She may never realize the wisdom that belongs to her.

Nine

Anima
The Woman In Every Man

One who has a man's wings
And a woman's also
Is in himself a womb of the world
And, being a womb of the world,
Continuously, endlessly,
Gives Birth (Laotzu, Tao Te Ching)

The woman that lives in the unconscious of every human male is referred to by Jung as the Anima. She is one of the most sought after properties in the unconscious but also one of the most elusive. This property, however, may not be bought for it already belongs to every man. It is his birthright.

In many cultures, it is the equivalent of owning a heavily mortgaged piece of property for which one may not collect any rents or rewards. Boys are not encouraged to express this side of their personalities lest they be labeled sissies. They are expected to act like "boys" and later like "men" no matter what. And so this property gains its elusive quality, for though it does exist in every man, he is not given any permits to develop it, and therefore it remains as dry and arid and non-productive as a piece of desert land. To take this property out of mortgage becomes essential to individuation and wholeness.

The relationship with the Anima often begins as the infamous midlife crisis. The man experiences symptoms. He cries more easily, feels vaguely senti-mental, moody; perhaps he feels a new and excited energy that feels like being in love but with what he isn't sure. There is a passion connected to the Anima that can frighten many a red-blooded man.

These feelings can be so disconcerting that an un-conscious man, one who is not willing to look within for answers, may feel strongly that his masculinity is being threatened. He sees this threat as coming from a woman and indeed it is, but rather than seeing that it is the woman within him, he may throw the blame onto the real outer woman or women in his life. This man begins to run amok, in flight from the pursuing feminine energy, typically to a new young naïve woman with whom he can reassert his masculinity, or to a new lifestyle or work where he can feel once again his full masculine power.

But the conscious man, the truly courageous man does not run. He faces her squarely and decides to make this property his own at whatever the cost. This ownership can only occur by first gaining awareness of the existence of such a property and through a willingness to add its energy to his assets, by giving it expression in his life.

What does this mean to a man? Why it is the step that moves him from a purely masculine one-sided way of being into a more open, receptive, creative, feeling way. His biggest fear, losing his masculinity, is more in danger by not allowing the feminine into his life than by accepting her with open arms. The reason for that is that she is there to compliment, to complete, and to give passion and warmth and openness to his being to make him a whole person.

And here is the place to say what a loving wife or partner does when her man has met and fallen in love with his Anima. She loves him more for there is now more of him to love.

What becomes of the man who neither flees nor faces his "inner-woman"? These men become what Jung called Anima possessed. They stay on the property without owning it; a tenant, living there paying high rent but without the benefits and rewards that ownership brings. They suffer moodiness, sentimentality, sometimes becoming old-womanish, shrewish and rather than using the available feminine energy to enlarge themselves, they diminish themselves, becoming less than they can be rather than more. Their manhood shrinks away and they are left in the possession of a frustrated inner woman who has not been allowed to breathe and live and so like a frustrated outer woman resorts to moody pouting, complaining, and nagging behavior in order to get some expression. It is never too late for a man to recognize this woman within him and to become intimate and related to her.

The big question becomes how does he relate to her? What does she want from him? I suppose in the end each man must discover this for himself, but it might help here to share the way that Dr. Jung himself approached the task.

Jung gave birth to this idea of the "woman within" mainly from his own experiences with her. In his autobiography Memories, Dreams, Reflections, Jung tells what happened while recording some of his fantasies in his journal:

> When I was writing down these fantasies, I once asked myself what am I really doing? Certainly this has nothing to do with science, but then 'what is it?' Whereupon a voice within me said 'It is art.' I was astonished it had never entered my head that what I was writing had any connection with art...I knew for a certainty that the voice had come from a woman. (Jung 1965)

Jung continued to write and the voice continued to confront him. He goes on to say that he was intrigued by the fact that a woman should interfere with him from within. He concluded she must be the soul in a primitive sense. He later saw that this inner feminine figure plays an archetypal role in the unconscious of a man and he called her the Anima.

She awed him. It felt like an invisible presence in the room. Then he realized that by writing his fantasies he was in effect writing letters to his Anima.

`He became like a patient in analysis with a ghost and a woman. Every evening he wrote to her as he realized this was the way for the Anima to get at his fantasies.

Jung was as honest as possible and wrote everything down carefully. As he wrote he had peculiar reactions that threw him off. He learned to separate himself from the interruption, which was the voice of the Anima.

In this way, writing to and dialoguing with this feminine voice within, Jung discovered his own Anima. Jung experienced this voice as an interruption and surely that is often how it feels. But as he continued his personal journey he came to see the positive Anima. He began to value her for the images of his unconscious, which she brought to him. He turned to her whenever he felt his emotional behavior was disturbed. He would ask her often what she was up to? What she sees? She regularly produced an image, which had the ability to dispel his sense of unrest and oppression. Instead, the negative energy was transformed into interest and curiosity about the image. He tried always to understand them just like a dream.

Of course Jung moved to a place of no longer needing the conversations with his Anima for he no longer had the disturbing emotions. But he said:

> *If I did have them, I would deal with them in the same way. Today I am directly conscious of the Anima's ideas because I have learned to accept the contents of the unconscious and to understand them. I know how I must behave toward the inner images. I can read their meaning directly from my dreams and I therefore no longer need a mediator to communicate them. (Jung 1965)*

From Jung's experience we see that one way for a man to begin to relate to his own Anima is to communicate with her both through the written and spoken word. Tell her your dreams and fantasies as well as your most secret thoughts. Begin a journal and think of it as your secret meeting place, the rendezvous between your inner woman and yourself.

The symbolic language of our dreams and fantasies is her native tongue. And you will soon find yourself in conversation with her. If, as Jung did, you go to her when your emotions are in upheaval, when you are feeling moody, and restless, you can directly ask her what she wants of you for at these times she is most present. With practice you will become alert to her response to you, usually in the form of an image (her language). Follow these images and you will soon be right again.

In his book Psyche Speaks, Jungian analyst and author, Russell Lockhart sheds more light on the subject. Referring to the same passage from Jung's autobiography, Lockhart says:

> *I want to point out that Jung asked a question of the psyche and got a straight answer. 'What am I really doing?' It is art. Any artist knows the driven quality the image moving toward birth brings. (Lockhart 1987)*

Lockhart later refers to a letter to Herbert Read where Jung refers to the Anima as the "mouthpiece" proclaiming the arrival of the coming guest. Lockhart continues:

> *The...spontaneous expression. 'It is art, 'perhaps this first Self-conscious expression of Anima as Anima in our time, hides an enormous meaning that we must attend to and not reject...It is a work that needs to be undertaken by each of us or we shall soon find ourselves splitting apart, fragmenting from one another and unable because of this to undertake the necessary task that lies before us. (Lockhart 1987)*

Lockhart suggests that receiving the images from the Anima is just the beginning. A man can best relate to her when he does something with the image. Pointing to Jung's journal writing he comments that it was "the act of writing it out" that was important, more than the scientific understanding Jung later gained.

So we see that while a first step must be to recognize the existence of the Anima. A man must then bring his manhood to her and this is best done through action. Lockhart suggests this can often be done by putting his "mood" into something concrete that he can see and experience. Painting, drawing, music, working with clay. etc. all serve the purpose well. Transforming his mood into his art. In this way he begins to understand the true value and friendship of this most noble part of himself.

In Sanford's book *The Invisible Partners*, he advises:

> *Men need to learn to talk with women and to listen to them, for a woman can instruct a man in what is important to her; in this way he becomes more related (to his feelings)...*

He continues:

> *A man in the grip of the Anima is for all the world like an inferior kind of woman which is upset about something and that, in fact, is exactly what he has become within himself...the antidote for this is for the man to know what he is feeling and become capable of expressing this in relationship. (Sanford 1980)*

Sanford advises men they can help themselves most by not turning away from the Anima.

Instead, a man who owns this property undergoes a new psychological development that includes the Anima and gives the man a "renewed respect for the world of the heart, for relationships, for the soul, and for the search for meaning. (Sanford 1980)

Ten

Animus
The Man in every woman,

It is a foregone conclusion among the initiated that men understand nothing of women's psychology as it actually is, but it is astonishing to find that women do not know themselves. (Jung 1970)

Getting to Know You

The property of the Animus is much like Rodeo Drive in Beverly Hills; a very rich property and our attitude about this property varies greatly depending upon our relationship to it. Much fear and trepidation arise as we approach. The best chance to own this property is by first becoming aware of its negative face. For when it is in possession of us, we will become moody and opinionated, filled with conviction. As von Franz stated, "When such conviction is preached with a loud, insistent, masculine voice or imposed on others by means of brutal emotional scenes, the underlying masculinity in a woman is easily recognized."

This chapter is very close to my heart. I have been in a love/hate relationship with my Animus most of my adult life. I love him when I am fully conscious and recognize him as my helper, my strength, my initiative, and my courage. I hate him when I have allowed him to possess me in some way and I am acting out completely against my will. At these times, I may even say afterward, 'I don't know what has gotten into me.' But while in its grip, I feel powerless to do anything but voice my opinions, and my judgments, which often may be right in a general way but are seldom appropriate to the situation I am in. The voice of the negative Animus is always cold, hard, and destructive. Von Franz writes one of its favorite themes repeated endlessly to a woman goes like this: "The only thing in the world that I want is love and he doesn't love me." Of course he doesn't if he is being presented with an unknown, opinionated male, the Animus. He may wonder, "Where has my woman gone?"

In our dreams, a man or a group of men, usually unknown to us, often represent the Animus. These dreams tell us we are on this property and give us the opportunity through recording and interpreting the dream to begin to see what he wants. The type of male images can hint at our stage of development. Later we will deal in detail with our dreams, (chapter fourteen) which along with our fantasies and our active imaginations are the pathways for meeting and befriending our Animus

It is the negative Animus of a woman most men dread meeting up with, comedians joke about, and which has given us our worst reputation as bitches, nags and shrews. And while we all hate these labels, is there a woman who has not experienced the possession of one of these aspects?

Men know there is no way for them to win in confrontation with the Animus, and feeling overwhelmed by its force, they often withdraw. Jung said, "This Animus is primitive man, and men want to react to it with their fists. But, as this is a woman, that way is barred to them, so they shun her." This serves to anger the woman even more for she is secretly wishing for this negative Animus energy to be stopped and a brave man will learn to stand up to it. (I suggest in a loving but firm way and tell it to stop). Humor is one of the best ways to break the spell.

Once a couple can both come to recognize the negative faces of the man's 'moody' Anima, and the woman's "opinionated" Animus, their relationship can take on a new dimension.

Sanford's book *Invisible Partners* deals with this subject in depth. He points out how the Animus keeps others from reaching a woman's warm and feeling side because they cannot get through the opinions of the Animus.

A child with an Animus-possessed mother can feel the lack of her affection as they keep coming up against the hard disciplinarian of the Animus with its critical, judgmental attitude instead of the tenderness and affection of the mother.

When the Animus is speaking to a woman, he is often telling her she is no good, a failure, ugly, fat, worthless. In the *Invisible Partners,* Sanford says, "When a woman gets a creative idea the Animus may say, 'You can't do that or other people can do these things much better than you.' Or, 'You have nothing of value to offer.' If she mistakes these words as her own thoughts the creative possibility is taken away from her."

Sanford suggests the term Animus:

> *...is a stiff term...but does not fit very well with the way he is actually experienced. When he is seen working within a woman's psyche it is often better to speak of him as the Great Prosecutor, the Top Sergeant, the Great Score Keeper, the Inner Judge. (Sanford 1980)*

What can a woman do to own this property and thereby break its hold on her? The answer is to give him what he wants. For as long as we do not recognize him he will never let up on us. What he wants is not that hard. He wants to be recognized and accepted as a beneficial partner. He is our male counterpart and has much to offer of a positive nature, but only if we do not sacrifice our womanhood to him. When he takes me over I not only sacrifice my femininity but I no longer relate in an authentic way. I get harsh, judgmental, and highly critical. And while I don't like myself at these times it seems impossible to stop. Only when I realize he needs an avenue of expression that includes my feminine nature, am I able to release his hold on me. My voice and my body get soft again, my heart warm and my creative juices flow.

He is my work! He is my masculine, creative energy. He simmers in every woman but she seldom gives him the opportunity to partner up and to be expressed. A woman seems to need a special kind of permission to develop this property. For to honor the man within she has to face the reality that she has work to do, a creative urge needing expression and that this work is as important for her as a woman as it is for any man.

A woman must believe deep within herself that her 'work' matters and she can only accomplish this by owning the Animus, setting him free in her life, befriending him, and using his energy as her own.

This work is not man's work or woman's work. It is however any work in which a woman brings her whole Self in a creative, energetic, and individual way. It can be seen in the baking of a cake, the raising of children, as well as the writing of a book or the painting of a picture. It may be in the world of business. But no matter what the work is, most importantly, both the man within and the woman must do it, for to sacrifice her womanhood is to become possessed by him.

In other words she must stop preaching her equal rights, she must instead experience this equality first within herself, by giving equal power to the man within. They must cohabit to her benefit. This is true liberation.

It is the Animus that can lead a woman to her soul. Sanford writes, "The Animus can appear to be demonic, yet in fact...he proves to be a relentless force that compels a woman to rid herself of weak, childish feelings and develop the true strength of her character."

To this day I can still be blindsided by my Animus. But gratefully I have the awareness of his existence and I can, through looking closely at what is going on in my life at that time as well as in my dreams, attempt to turn his energy to a positive use. For myself I have discovered that Animus often appears when my little girl is activated within, when my feelings are hurt or I am feeling weak and not well in some way. What I've learned at these times is I am needing a "daddy" to care for and protect me. Animus appears instead, sword in hand to defend me from further hurt. Thankfully I know enough now to take responsibility for how I am feeling, take the blame off of others, and turn the Animus energy into a positive and creative one. I thank him for coming to my rescue. This isn't easy. And the journey for each person is different.

I am writing this book in partnership with the Animus. It is he that gives me the bridge to my intellect, shines a light on what I know and gives me the courage to speak. It is also the Animus, in partnership with my thinking and sensation functions that has given me the focused attention and concentration to stay with this work.

It is a partnership because I have recognized this energy in myself and have received his input in a warm feeling, non-threatened way. For he could not have life without my willingness and receptiveness. I think of him as the blood and bones of the writing and my feminine side as the breath and inspiration.

The following exercises offer physical clues to recognize this property. Through awareness and practice he can become your most valuable asset.

1. LISTEN FOR THE CHANGE IN YOUR VOICE.

When you hear yourself going from soft and feminine to harsh, strident, and dictatorial STOP! Become aware of the change and gain back control of your own voice. If you have become permanently harsh and lacking in warmth, you have become possessed by the Animus. In other words, he is running the show and you are doing his dance. To regain control, try not talking as much. Instead pick up a pencil or colored pen or piece of clay and put his voice into these objects.

2. LISTEN FOR OPINIONS, ACCUSATIONS, and SUSPICIONS.

When you hear words coming from your mouth that even you recognize as not right or appropriate and find yourself cringing even while you are spewing forth, the Animus is trying hard to get your attention. Listen also to the negative Self-defeating voice within telling you that you are no good, ugly, unloved, unworthy, and untalented. Visualize this voice as coming from an angry little boy trying to get your attention. Love him and tell him you recognize he is frustrated and find the ways to redirect his energy.

While doing my writing he often tells me I am stupid and do not know anything. I now have a page just for him and instead of letting him stop my work, I write his comments on a page of their own. Pretty soon he stops. I think he becomes satisfied that I have noticed him and now he can become a true partner in my work. A later reading of his remarks is extremely helpful in learning to recognize the voice of the negative animus as separate from my Self. He is only calling out, not to hurt me, but ultimately to help me.

3. WATCH FOR RIGIDITY IN YOUR BODY.

Hard bodies may be in, but rigid, tense muscle-culture belongs to your Animus. As you find yourself tensing, breathe deeply, shrug and release your shoulders and be conscious each time the Animus gains control. Kindly but firmly release his control over you.

4. COMMUNICATE.

When my Animus has taken hold of me I find it very useful to journal with him. I ask him directly "what do you want?" Keep the conversation going as long as you can. You'll be surprised how clear, concise, and willing he can be.

5. RECORD YOUR DREAMS.

This is an excellent daily practice and will enable you to recognize the Animus as he appears in your dreams. This is the truest look at this property. He may be in the form of a man, or group of men, a boy or group of boys, most often unknown to you, very frequently a burglar or intruder or hostile male figures. Also, look for any male figure representing the various stages of the Animus development. Keeping track of him through your dreams will soon enlighten you about his real demands on you. In this way you will gradually bring him out of the unconscious and into the light of day.

By giving him his own voice and recognizing what he is saying, you will be lifting him out of unconsciousness, differentiating him and, allowing him to mature and work with you instead of against you. Think of beauty embracing the beast. In this way you will become true allies on your journey to Individuation.

Eleven

The Wise Old Man and
The Wise Old Woman

*There is a bewildering thing in human life; that the
thing that causes the greatest fear is the source of the
greatest wisdom. One's greatest foolishness is one's
biggest stepping-stone. (Jung)*

*No one can become a wise man (or woman) without be-
ing a terrible fool. (Jung 1928)*

The wise old man and the wise old woman are
archetypal images that are the least known to the
vast majority of people. Science fiction author Isaac
Asimov said, "The saddest aspect of life right now is
that science gathers knowledge faster than society
gathers wisdom." And while his observation was
years ago, it seems to have gotten worse.

What exactly is wisdom? We all have some idea of
what wisdom is. In a group of one hundred people

each might have a totally different definition but most would agree that it has something to do with doing the right thing, knowing what the right thing is, being able to conduct your life in a way that stands apart and above the norm.

Dictionaries cite understanding, which includes empathy and compassion as well as comprehension. It also includes knowledge, (not purely academic) common sense, insight, perception, accumulated learning, and real life experience. But as I see it, one might actually have all of these traits and still not act wisely. A life in search of meaning and purpose gathers the components but like a thousand piece jigsaw puzzle one must fit the pieces together to complete the picture. We might have much accumulated learning and life experience but fail to apply our common sense in approaching problems or dealing with others. Or if ego takes pride in our knowledge or we believe ourselves to be the most understanding of people, over all others, this too will show a lack of wisdom.

Wisdom is a complex concept. Yet we all seem able to recognize wisdom when we meet it in life. Those people we most admire and choose as mentors exhibit wisdom. For me obviously Jung was a wisdom figure, but so also was my grandmother. When I asked her what makes happiness, she replied, "Happiness, not with money. It helps because you have anything you want to have, but it doesn't make you happy. You are true to one another, you believe in one another and you are healthy. You got your health and you got everything. If you are sick, you are not happy. When I had pneumonia, I was on my deathbed. They called my mother and father to come and say goodbye, but I fooled them. I don't know what it is. I'm not a quitter. If they don't quit me, I don't quit them." Grandma was simple, grandma was basic, and she had abundant common sense which often translates into wisdom.

Well-known wisdom figures from the Bible, mythology, and contemporary life abound. The list of wise men and women is so familiar to most people they can be known by one name. Lincoln, Edison, Angelou, Jung, Mandala, Jefferson, Gandhi, King, Newton, Plato, Einstein, Aristotle, Socrates. From the Bible we have Solomon, Moses and Sophia. Two of my favorites are Anne Frank who said, "The final forming of a person's character lies in their own hands" and Helen Keller, "I am only one; but still I am one. I cannot do everything, but still I can do something, I will not refuse to do the something I can do."

They both exhibited much wisdom even at early ages. This follows Oprah Winfrey's advice, "Turn your wounds into wisdom." It is not how wisdom is earned and accumulated but how we use and apply it to real life situations that benefit us as well as our fellow human beings.

Sometimes I can feel the wise old woman and the wise old man helping me when I most need it, but if I believe myself to be wise and act from my ego, I fall into a trap. Wisdom can work in my life only when I get out of the way. Socrates said, "The only true wisdom is in knowing you know nothing."

Words of Wisdom from Wise sources can help us but wisdom cannot be easily taught. Instead one must be in relationship with the action verbs associated with wisdom; such as: grow, gather, perceive, detect, acquire, discover, gain. These words imply an active participation on our own part if we are to become wise.

We can grow in wisdom most during times of transition in our lives. At these times we may be deeply searching for some guidance from a higher power. We may be feeling lost and without direction and this is where the Wise Old Woman and the Wise Old Man property/archetypes may help us by making appearances in our dreams. They bring with them help from our accumulated life experience, our knowledge, our insights, and our understanding. They warn us of danger; they help us to make good decisions.

How can we recognize these figures in our dreams? The Wise Old Man often appears in the form of Clergymen, Doctors, Ministers, Gurus, Teachers, Magicians, Wizards, Prophets, as well as Fathers and Grandfathers. He will appear as someone older than we are.

Wise Old Woman appears often as a Grandmother, a Goddess, a Queen, Teacher, Therapist, or any older woman radiating authority and who has come to offer guidance and wisdom gathered from our personal and cultural experiences.

In searching through my dream journals, one of the earliest visits from Wise Old Man in my dreams came at a time of great transition for me. I was ending my failed marriage, beginning my career in Real Estate and starting my journey into Jungian Analysis.

In my dream I was sick and consulted a doctor who diagnosed me with bowel cancer. He said going east to Notre Dame could cure me. I noted when I awoke that I had a feeling of excitement at the possibility of a new venture. Working with the images in the dream I later interpreted it as follows. The bowel cancer represented to me something eating at me at a very deep level; the direction East has many symbolic meanings. For me what resonated was the rising of the sun in the east and the entrance to the Garden of Eden, which faced east. They represented to me the birth of consciousness. Notre Dame symbolized a spiritual life and all this was delivered by the Wise Old Man in the image of the doctor who told me I could be cured. That essentially started me on my life-long search for wisdom and spirituality, which, believe me, still can be elusive, but has been a very worthy pursuit.

To be able to understand and earn the wisdom of the dream, we may need to heed the wise words of Jungian and Mythologist, Joseph Campbell. "We must be willing to let go of the life we planned so as to have the life that is waiting for us." At times of transition, wisdom is often asking us to let go of the familiar habits and ways of being that continue to hurt us, in favor of what may feel very unfamiliar and uncomfortable but can speed our growth. Wisdom can help us to make good choices. I have found wisdom in the song lyrics, "You gotta know when to hold them and know when to fold them," by Kenny Rogers. Seems very simple but how often do we hang on past the point of gaining any good from a situation and ending up with regret for having stayed too long.

Following a path of wisdom takes courage. How much easier is it to try to change another person then it is to change ourselves? In my life my second marriage got much better once I became wise enough to realize that I was the one that needed to change. Once I made significant alterations in my attitudes as well as my actions and my expectations, my husband miraculously changed for the better as well and our relationship deepened. Acquiring wisdom means letting go of the unwise ways we have been living.

As far back as the Bible, wisdom was a topic:

> *How blessed is the man who finds wisdom, and the man who gains understanding. For its profit is better*

*than the profit of silver, and its gain than of fine gold.
She is more precious than jewels; and nothing you desire compares with her. Long life is in her right hand;
in her left hand are riches and honor. Her ways are
pleasant ways and all her paths are peace. She is a tree
of life to those who take hold of her, and happy are all
who hold her fast." (Proverbs 3:1)*

The goddess of wisdom, Sophia, was said to be the soul of God. Much like Anima is the soul of a man.

One of China's greatest philosophers and teachers, Confucius, was born in 551 BC and his wisdom has survived through the ages. He said, "Life is really simple, but we insist on making it complicated." And "It does not matter how slowly you go as long as you do not stop."

Wisdom is gathered slowly through a lifetime and requires patience. It is earned when we make our life our work. It is not easily taught except from our own mistakes and by the acute observer and student of the mistakes and failings made by others. Once we recognize this property and open ourselves to its miraculous gifts we may trip and fall from time to time but through wisdom we will know how to pick ourselves up and move forward. For in the end wisdom is one of the best friends we could ever hope to have.

Wisdom Quotes

"By three methods we may learn wisdom. First by reflection, which is noblest. Second by imitation, which is easiest. Third through experience, which is bitterest." Confucius

"Friendship with oneself is all-important, because without it one cannot be friends with anyone else in the world." Eleanor Roosevelt

"Knowledge speaks, but wisdom listens." Jimi Hendricks

"Any fool can know; the point is to understand." Einstein

"The fool doth think he is wise, but the wise man knows himself to be a fool." Shakespeare, As *You Like It*

"The only true wisdom is in knowing you know nothing." Socrates

"Kindness to others is the only rent we pay for our room on Earth." Muhammad Ali

"If you are always trying to be normal you will never know how amazing you can be." Maya Angelou.

"Knowing yourself is the beginning of all wisdom." Aristotle

"There is only one way to avoid criticism - do nothing, say nothing and be nothing." Aristotle

"A wise man can learn more from a foolish question then a fool can learn from a wise answer." Bruce Lee

"Patience is the companion of wisdom." Saint Augustine

"Trust yourself. Create the kind of Self that you will be happy to live with your whole life. Make the most of yourself by fanning the tiny, inner sparks of possibility into flames of achievement." Golda Meir

"Well done is better than well said." Benjamin Franklin

"We can easily forgive a child who is afraid of the dark; the real tragedy of life is when men are afraid of the light." Plato

"When I do good I feel good when I do bad I feel bad - that is my religion." Abraham Lincoln

"Those who do not know how to weep with their whole heart don't know how to laugh either" Golda Meir

"I learned that courage was not the absence of fear, but the triumph over it. The brave man is not he who does not feel afraid, but he who conquers that fear." Nelson Mandela

"I have not failed. I just found 10,000 ways that won't work." Thomas Edison

"Be happy in each moment, that's enough. Each moment is all we need, no more." Mother Teresa

"Even if you're on the right track, you'll get run over if you just sit there." Will Rogers

"If you don't like the road you're a walking, start paving another one." Dolly Parton

"If you bring forth what is within you, what you bring forth will save you. If you do not bring forth what is within you, what you do not bring forth will destroy you." Gospel of Thomas

"I choose to make the rest of my life the best of my life." Louise Hay

"Wisdom is not a product of schooling but of the life-long attempt to acquire it." Einstein

"And the day came when the risk to remain tight in a bud was more painful than the risk it took to blossom." Anais Nin

"Do unto others as you would have done unto you." Jesus

Part Two

Building
a
Tool Chest

Twelve

Road Blocks

JAIL

Incarceration: Terror is the best of guards (anon)

Before we begin using the tools we need to also recognize common roadblocks along the way. Growth in life comes best through times of trouble. When however, we get stuck in a bad place we feel imprisoned. This is the result of a subtle construction of our own prison cells and represents a major obstacle on the road to individuation. The light has dimmed and we have temporarily lost touch with the outside world.

It may help to envision this condition as being in a holding cell. Normal life is for the time being suspended. A protective wall around our psyche has locked us in, in a mistaken effort to keep pain out. We can go for many years without realizing that our fortress has become our prison. Life will remain suspended until we see that the pain we are living with daily is greater than the pain we have gone to great lengths to avoid.

Fortunately, life provides the way out of jail. It requires our full awareness and must be undertaken by the builder of the jail, our ego. To gain our freedom, our ego first must accept responsibility for our imprisonment. Through its pursuit of supremacy over our lives our ego builds the walls around us block by block. Well-meaning in its wish to protect us from pain, our ego now must let go of the anger, fear and resentment it uses to control our lives.

Many short-timer jail stays necessarily occur in our lifetimes when our ego attempts to keep both the inner and the outer worlds away from us. At these times we are caught between two opposites poles. We feel as though there is no way out and in fact freedom does not lie with either one or the other of these two choices. Instead, the task of rehabilitation is accomplished through recognizing the two opposing sides and finding a way to bring them into the light.

These short time stays are difficult to recognize because while we are caught between two opposite and conflicting attitudes or ways of being, we are only able to see the conscious one in the outer world. The other, inner attitude is still hidden within our unconscious and so we are not able to be aware of the true nature of our dilemma. This creates a genuine fight within us.

The way out of jail and back into life comes through uniting of the opposites, which births a new option, one we had never before considered. It is not compromise; it is letting go of the fear, anger, and resentment which have effectively locked us up.

While we are not conscious of being locked in the jail property we will continue to struggle vainly.

Often we have ignored the clues, which are being delivered to us nightly in our dreams. In these dreams we may be in chains, locked in a room, or any similar situation where we find ourselves trapped and unable to get out. We think that by shaking ourselves awake from what we call our nightmare, we will be free from the predicament, but this is in fact a delusion.

The unconscious is ever present and persistent and it will try in every way it has available to get our attention. At this time it is crucial to pay attention to our dreams and fantasies, which can be counted on to supply a clear picture of the problem and a solution as well. Our conscious minds need a symbol to bring the opposites together and symbols are exactly what our dreams provide.

When the path is not clear and we may be hitting our heads against invisible walls or walking in circles in the small space we have carved out for ourselves, we have probably become prisoners. Hopelessness and the feeling that there is no way out are the common symptoms of a jailbird. At these times we must be willing to risk a prison break, even though what lies ahead is unknown and terrifying. Taking the risk in spite of our fear is the quickest way to remove the bars.

As an example, let's look at a person who is spending life in a one-sided, outgoing, extroverted way always surrounded by people, activity and commotion. He begins to suffer the symptoms of an inmate, restless, discontented, but still does not know what the problem is.

He no longer enjoys being the center of the action, in fact it now has become a burden, and life is not bringing him the satisfaction it once did. He has no idea what the matter is and cannot find the answer in his everyday life.

Meanwhile, deep within his unconscious lives his introverted opposite. This quiet, more withdrawn aspect of himself, urgently wants to have life too, but since this man's greatest fear is that of being left alone and quiet, he has never even considered allowing this introverted side of himself to exist. So there they both sit, in jail.

One night he dreams he is at a large party. There are people everywhere, music and loud noise. And there he sits in the center of it all, but his arms and legs are bound and he is helpless to get free. No one in the room seems to notice that he is struggling.

He shakes himself awake, cold sweat covering his body. The next day he still cannot forget the dream of the night before and for the first time in his life he contemplates what the dream might be telling him. He suddenly sees that in some way he is a prisoner in life. This awareness alone begins to make him feel somewhat better for now he can use the symbol of being tied up to see how it applies to his real life.

Very shortly he is rewarded with another dream. This time he is all alone in a beautiful park, drawing a picture of a flower. It's a completely relaxing dream and in it he feels a superb sense of freedom. This is the kind of dream he doesn't want to wake up from but when he does he feels strangely euphoric.

Continuing to take the symbols of his dreams seriously he suddenly realizes in a flash of understanding that maybe he needs to get off by himself in a natural setting and see if he can capture the feeling of the dream in his "real" life. This is an entirely unfamiliar idea to this fellow. Yet he seems to have a new feeling about being alone and is not as afraid of the idea as he has always been before.

Through some patient work, watching his dreams and following the clues they present to him he eventually finds the way to bring his more introverted counterpart into his life, thereby creating out of the opposites, a new entity; a person who is dominated neither by the one always seeking the company of others, nor the one who sits alone in withdrawal, but rather one free to be with others or alone as he needs to be, giving life to both and bringing them together for his personal betterment.

Of course the solutions our dreams bring to us are different for each person and we must come to recognize the language spoken in own inner world.

We may find ourselves a prisoner of our own thinking and unable to easily access our feelings. As a result we feel something is missing and are not sure what. We are stuck. If we journey into the unconscious through our dreams and fantasies, a unifying symbol can appear which if taken seriously can lead us to relationship with the previously hidden feeling side, thereby bringing wholeness and greater well-being. The fear that our previously held feelings have kept us imprisoned, causes more damage than actually feeling our feelings could ever have done.

I once dreamt of tears in my ears, which became a symbol to me of unshed tears and ever after made me more receptive to staying in touch with feelings of sadness. This is difficult work but so incredibly rewarding, that once begun there will be no stopping. In time we will be merely a visitor to jail for we will always know where the keys to the cell door can be found.

There is still another kind of jail. This one is built by the culture and environment in which we are living and sometimes by fate. The outer walls of this structure may never come down, but the person who gains mastery in the process of individuation finds an inner way to freedom.

I am reminded here of the remarkable diaries of Anne Frank. Locked into a prison, not of her own making, we are privileged to view a spirit nonetheless free through the pages of her writing. And Helen Keller, prisoner in sightless, speechless, and deaf body freed her spirit in this life and touched and inspired millions. While both of these women raged at times against their imprisonment neither of them ever lost their spirit to it.

At twelve, Helen Keller wrote, "My life is full of happiness. Every day brings me some new joy, some fresh token of love from distant friends" and later "I seldom think about my limitations, and they never make me sad... Perhaps there is just a touch of yearning at times; but it is vague, like a breeze among flowers.

Thirteen

Bankruptcy — Foreclosure

Bankrupt: A person who is totally lacking in a specified resource or quality: an intellectual bankrupt.

Foreclosure Middle English forclosen, to exclude from an inheritance, From Old French forclos, shut out, past participle of forclore, to exclude: fors-, outside

These are dreaded words to our capitalist ears and definitely an obstacle to our progress. In real terms this condition comes about from spending more than we have or improper use of our resources. A lack of balance, of thriftiness and most often a lack of consciousness is the root cause. It is fueled by the ego, whose favorite line is "I want it and I want it now".

Psychologically speaking, in order to fall into this state we have ignored the voice of our inner partners that almost always can be counted on to give us a warning of impending danger.

We become needy and our suffering, unconscious ego will go to any length to fill the perceived need. It can stem from loneliness, insecurity, hunger of all kinds, for all things, jealousy, feelings of inadequacy, etc. Our unconscious ego spends all it has of its own limited resources to stop the pain, and to get its needs met right now at any cost.

We need just to view the bankrupt lives of drug addicts, alcoholics, shopaholics, love addicts, food addicts, and all with the "more, more, more," psychology. The common denominator is some form of addiction, which soon creates the problem of over-spending our resources in an effort to fill the emptiness within. One day life will call for payment in full and when we cannot pay, foreclosure and bankruptcy are the remedies. For Jung, "Every form of addiction is bad, no matter whether the narcotic be alcohol, morphine or idealism."

In our western society, unfortunately, bankruptcy is the savior. We get to start again with a clean slate, while our creditors do not get paid. But unless we undergo a deep and abiding change of consciousness and seek out professional help and therapies, mental, physical and material, we will probably be back into bankruptcy as soon as we are eligible.

Owning our inner properties is the way to avoid this condition. They are there to help us, but we must stop looking for instant gratification and instead be willing to tolerate the pain or suffering of the moment long enough to tune in to messages coming from within: in the form of dreams, symbols, fantasies, and becoming familiar with the way in which they are trying to communicate with us.

Our inner properties are our bank to which we all hold a passbook. Here are the resources and "savings" meant to save us. An image comes to mind of an old, sick, miser, who dies a miserable and lonely death only to have it be discovered that he had buried his wealth for years in the ground. This does not have to be our fate. The riches buried within us can never be fully spent. The more we draw on them the greater they grow.

Fourteen

Dreams

"Nights through dreams tell the myths forgotten by the day."   (Jung 1963)

One of the most effective tools available for locating our inner properties, and developing them to their highest potential in our lives, are the ever-forthcoming dreams delivered from the unconscious. They serve as clues, warnings, prognosticators, and can reveal the wealth of inner properties awaiting discovery.

Jung wrote, "A dream unanalyzed is like a letter unopened." Many of us think nothing of tossing unopened junk mail into the trash, but it is essential to the development of your inner properties that the messages our dreams send to us not be treated with this same casual disregard. Yet, this is a commonplace occurrence.

Some claim not to dream at all. These people just have not learned the route to the post office. The mail is there, being delivered every day, but they must pick it up. There are others that remember their dreams intermittently, especially the big dreams. These are dreams that are so extraordinary in their content and so removed from the realm of our daily existence that one cannot help but notice. Yet they go no further than noticing. They examine the envelope carefully, comment on how it looks, and then toss it away.

Some people dream the same dream over and over again. Every good salesman knows that by sending the same letter out repeatedly the statistics show a person will stop throwing it away and actually read it. If the salesman persists they may even make the sale. Dreams that come to us more than one time may be considered as urgent messages that will keep coming until we treat them seriously by asking what the dream wants from us.

Once aware of the value inherent in our dream communications, the life we live will be changed in dramatic ways. We now no longer rely on chance or luck to survive. We are now able to acquire true skill in life and will baffle those who have not discovered this entree to the unconscious.

The study and analysis of dreams and fantasies, as well as myths and fairy tales, formed the basis of Jung's psychological system. Once he had discovered that the world we are conscious of in our waking moments was only a small island, he became intrigued with what lay below the level of the water in that vast sea of the unconscious that exists unseen and unknown in each of us. His life's mission became the exploration of the contents of his own unconscious. The only way he could gain entry to that world was by learning the language spoken there. It is not English, Japanese, French, Italian, Greek or Latin.

Symbolism is the language of this hidden world. And these symbols are presented to us daily through the messages of our dreams and fantasies. Until this is discovered, we operate in life with a most severe handicap.

Imagine driving a car with no rear or side view mirrors, no road signs, traffic signals or street markings. All we can rely on is what we see immediately in front of us. We would not get any further than the first intersection before we encountered chaos, confusion, uncertainty and helplessness.

This is the same result of a life lived without the help and guidance of the unconscious and its gifts to us delivered nightly in the form of our dreams. Yet this blind way of living is a most popular and accepted way.

It is not easy for us to interpret our own dreams for the fact that they are coming from our unconscious. This means we have a blind spot to them. Jung said:

> *I have noticed that dreams are as simple or as compli-*
> *cated as the dreamer is himself, only they are always a*
> *little bit ahead of the dreamer's consciousness. I do not*
> *understand my own dreams any better than any of*
> *you, for they are always somewhat beyond my grasp*
> *and I have the same trouble with them as anyone who*
> *knows nothing about dream interpretation. Knowledge*
> *is no advantage when it is a matter of ones own*
> *dreams. (Jung 1939)*

In the *Way of The Dream* by Fraser Boa, von Franz offers the following help for interpreting one's own dreams:

> *In Jungian psychology, we have a technique. We com-*
> *pare the dream to a drama and examine it under three*
> *headings: first the introduction, the setting of the*
> *dream, and the naming of the problem." Starting here*
> *you make your own associations to these items of place,*
> *time and persons, asking yourself questions such as*
> *'How did I feel there? Was I happy? What is that per-*
> *son like?*
>
> *Second, the.... ups and downs of the story; and finally,*
> *the end solution perhaps, catastrophe. (Boa with von*
> *Franz 1992)*

She suggests if we are interpreting our own dreams that we write them on one side of a paper and for every word, write our associations to that word opposite. In this way we can make a connection between our dream and our waking associations.

She cites as example that if a dream takes place in our childhood home, we may associate a way in which we are still childlike. A dream of a burglar might give us the association of something breaking into our consciousness. This then could connect us to an event and eventually we might have the "Aha" moment when we realize something right or wrong about our behavior and in this way it corrects our attitude.

In his book Inner Work, Robert Johnson covers these same steps to interpreting our own dreams in great detail and adds a fourth step: Ritual. He suggests that after we have done our best to understand the dream with our mind, the fourth step is to do something physical.

When I dreamt of seeing an intricate and beautiful painting whose artist signature turned out to be mine, I signed up for my first drawing class and while I have never reached the perfection of that dream painting, I have been drawing and painting with a great amount of pleasure and reward ever since and cannot imagine my life without this added partner. Johnson says in this way we can integrate our dream experience into our conscious, waking life. If this step seems difficult he assures us that with a little practice we can invent ingenious rituals that will give our dreams physical concreteness. This step can intensify our understanding of the dream and, he says, can even change our habits and attitudes.

He gives a wonderful example of a young college student he was working with in analysis who dreamt he was out in a shopping center on Saturday night. Everything went badly. Junk food made him sick and superficial acquaintanceships left him unsatisfied. He interpreted that the dream referred to the way he spent Saturday nights: going out with the guys, drinking a lot, eating unhealthy food all left him feeling empty afterward.

Johnson asked him "What did you do about your dream?"

The student answered, 'I went to a hamburger stand and bought the biggest deluxe cheeseburger and an order of French fries and with a high, solemn ceremony I buried it.' He did this as a symbolic act of renunciation. He ritually affirmed his intention to give up the superficial and destructive involvements that the dream had called to his attention.

"The ritual cured him of seeking nourishment where it could not be found, of giving his life over to people and activities that could not feed him on any deep level." (Johnson 2009)

There are other dreams to which people generally have no personal associations they can make. They have a mythological meaning. In these cases we take the associations of mankind. The symbols in these dreams are best found in studies of mythologies, fairy tales, folklore and religious imagery. These are the "collective representations that come from primeval dreams and creative fantasies".

On a trip to the Jung Institute in Switzerland, I had a dream of standing on top of a mountain and encountering a large brown bear. He forced me to the edge and as I went over he swiped the bottom of my foot, leaving a large mark. I fell gently down and ended by going through a prism of light.

I knew upon waking that this was not one of my everyday dreams. I actually could feel the mark on the "soul" of my foot. The dream stayed with me long after my return home and in order to work on it, I began to seek out explanations of the symbol of the bear.

I can still remember these many years later, the shock of discovery when I read of the cave bears whose skulls were found deep in the caves of the Swiss Alps and were the evidence of the earliest religion known to man, that of the Neanderthal. My amazement grew when I discovered that these skulls were in the museum in Basel, Switzerland, the birthplace of Jung and the place I was visiting.

This dream opened many doors for me and in effect started me on my own personal journey through the prism of light and my adventures into the world of art and color. There is a saying that when the student is ready the teacher shall appear. This dream certainly became my teacher.

Franz, in Way Of The Dream states that she does not believe dream dictionaries are particularly helpful. "The dream symbolism…is much more individual. What's important is always what the symbol means to the dreamer and what the dreamer has experienced with it."

From the dream above one can see that it was important for me to find what meaning the bear held for me as a symbol in my psyche. I had to work for it but it certainly was worth the effort. There are however some general themes, such as falling, dying, giving birth, and being chased. Franz says about the latter:

> In general, if something in the dream pursues us it wants to come to us. But by being afraid of it we lend it an evil figure. If only we could face up to this side of our nature and accept it, it would probably become more benevolent. (Boa with von Franz 1992)

I would like to conclude with a dream von Franz uses to illustrate:

> I remember a man who had great gifts in writing and who should have written his thesis for the Jung Institute. He had dreams that powerful animals pursued him, which I interpreted as his creativity wanting to reach him. But he didn't want to write and couldn't write until he dreamt that a bull pursued him. He ran and ran, and the bull was after him, coming closer and closer, until at the last minute he jumped over a fence.

The bull stood still and went onto his hind legs. And the dreamer looked back and saw the erect penis of the bull, and it was a ballpoint pen. So I said, 'Well there you are.' After that he wrote an excellent thesis. (Boa with von Franz 1992)

Dreams provide a lifelong guide to the vast terrain of the unconscious and the chance to connect to the many properties begging for your ownership. Here we can uncover our shadow, our mask, our Anima, Animus, our inner child, mother, father, the trickster, and the multitude of fascinating aspects to our psyche that await discovery and the chance to make us into the whole, individuated human we are meant to be.

Tips for remembering your dreams.

Many people believe that they never dream or they have great difficulty remembering their dreams. In our busy world today I think it's due to the fact that we go to bed with a mind that can't shut down the internal chatter. We mull over problems, plan the next day's activities and relive the day's events. But be assured, scientific sleep studies do validate that we all dream, not only once but several times a night, approximately ninety minutes apart.

So how can we reconnect to our dream life? There is generally a consensus among analysts and other dream workers that the following steps aid greatly.

Don't give up. Dream recall can be likened to an underused muscle. The more you use it the stronger it becomes and with practice you will be lifting large portions of dream material from your unconscious. Be patient with your Self and have fun with the process. A desperate approach never works.

1. The first, important step is to set an intention to remember. You must want to. By suggesting to yourself your desire to remember and following up with other preparatory steps, you will be putting out the welcome mat to your unconscious.

I can go for long stretches without remembering my dreams, but when I am in times of stress, worry, unhappiness, or just uncomfortable and indecisive, I turn to my dreams for help If distractions in my home, my present schedule, or any other domestic disturbance - including my cats waking me at 5:30 to eat - keep me from fully committing to my dreams, I take a "dream" vacation. A few days away from home with the firm intention to remember my dreams can do wonders.

2. Strive for a regular time to go to bed and to wake up.

A set routine and a positive attitude can help a great deal. If possible, do not set an alarm. If you must, use the gentlest one you can find.

3. Drinking alcohol or eating rich foods too close to bedtime can inhibit dreaming.

4. Keep pencil and notebook or a recorder next to your bed so that the means to record your dream will be within reach as soon as you wake up. I have, for years, kept a notebook next to my bed. I like to use a special one that becomes a part of my dream journals. I can look back later at a dream that may not have meant anything to me at the time but ended up having great significance. Even if I wake in the middle of the night I write down a word or two or any image, no matter how small, before going back to sleep. Today with technologies and our smart phones it has become even easier to record them. Whether you write these fragments or record them always use the present tense i.e. "I am in a forest, it is very dark, and I am frightened . . ." Write your free association with the individual words and images.

5. In the morning, try to wake slowly, lay still and keep your eyes closed and move as little as possible. This is the time to try to capture the feeling you have awoken with. Is it frustration (lost something and can't find it), scary (you are being chased), warm and fuzzy (sharing a good meal with friends) Can you describe the setting?

6. Write down as many details as you can remember, no matter how small. This is not the time to critique the content. The silliest appearing dream can be the most profound. If an image is particularly strong and you want to draw it, by all means do so. One picture can sometimes open the door wider than words. Interpretation can and should be left for later.

7. Share your dreams as a way of acknowledging they are important to you. This will make them more real and keep them longer in your consciousness.

8. If you can make some aspect of the dream manifest in your life do it. Can you draw it? Sculpt it? Act it out in some way.

9. Dream recall is like weight training. It is a muscle, which with time and practice can be strengthened. Be patient and kind to yourself. Even a single word, image or sensation should be noted for it can open wide to a new world.

In my early dream notebooks I dreamt and noted the mouth of a cave. It took two years to dream of entering the cave but ended up signaling the beginning of my personal journey to my own unconscious. In subsequent dreams over the next years I descended deeper and deeper. By keeping my dream journals I have been able to track my progress. Leave room on the pages for drawings, notes, or any ideas that occur. Just like a photo can bring you back to a time, a place and a feeling, looking through my dream journals reconnects me to important transitions in my life.

Enjoy your journey

Fifteen

Wu Wei

The Art of Not Doing

When our involvement in the world becomes
overwhelming, as it is certain to do, there
awaits for us a property that resembles a plot of
vacant land. There is a mentality, which one may
clearly observe in action here in the great city of Los
Angeles, that says no land may sit vacant. There exists
an irresistible urge to fill every space. In Real Estate
there is a concept that all land should be used to its
highest and best use. But who among us can make
that judgment?

I have been fortunate enough to live beside a lovely and deep ravine. The emptiness of it, the lack of
human population, has been a great source of peace
for me and has enabled me to continue to live in this
fast-paced, ever-developing city.

Now our community is engaged in a battle with developers to preserve the ravines and bluffs as the natural home they are to owls, hawks, possums, rabbits, squirrels, plants of all description, and as a place for children to explore and get to know the nature of their world. The reality is that this land is not vacant. It is teeming with life, though it is life that only some eyes can see.

A landscape architect at one of our community meetings speaks of our ravines as living things, and "sees" the life there. He talks to us of healing the land. He wants to put back the natural shrubs and trees and grasses of this environment and calls on the people who have lived here to remember it as it was. Where he has been free to do this nearby, the entire balance of the area is restoring itself.

By replanting the buckwheat plants the blue butterflies soon returned. Each restoration of a native plant brought with it the return of the indigenous wildlife. We were being overrun with gophers but as the natural plant life was reintroduced, the gopher snakes and hawks, which are the natural predators of the gopher, soon returned.

In each of us there is a wilderness. It too teems with life but just as in the world, we do not always have the eyes to see. Our egos act as the developer who cannot stand the anxiety of seeing the emptiness. The developers in and of themselves, are not the problem. It is their intention that matters. Is the motivation coming from the ego wanting more and more money, fame, and land or is the urge coming from their spirit wanting to fulfill its purpose?

It is only when we stop greedily filling every so-called empty moment of our lives that we begin to see the vacant places with new eyes. It is imperative for this inward journey that we stop at least once in a day to sit quietly in the emptiness, observing our anxiety but not giving in to it. This is an effective tool for the tool chest. One that allows us to see the life that exists within. As we heal and restore our wounded and scarred interior landscapes, we too create the natural environment in which the inner properties can thrive.

In the same way that vacant land is not vacant, "Not Doing" is not doing "nothing." It is instead jumping boldly into the flow of life and swimming effortlessly, without acting, controlling, or willing the movement. It is being in the zone – going with the flow. This is action of a different kind. It is action of the spirit in which our egos must let go of directing, pushing, motivating, and acting in favor of letting the Spirit within and the rhythms of life take over. It means cooperating with the natural flow, which leads to freedom and independence.

Wu Wei is not being separate from life but rather connected in the deepest way. It is not being a couch potato or a passive observer of life, or even a sitter on a cushion all day, but rather the opposite. By swimming in the ever-moving flow of life we are connected to all of life.

George Mumford, author of *The Mindful Athlete, The Secrets to Pure Performance,* understands Wu Wei masterfully. He describes being in the zone as "no sense of I, me, or mine, no actor, nobody doing it... The best way to get into the zone is not to try to get into the zone."

He has aided many peak performing athletes, such as Michael Jordan and Kobe Bryant. After Mumford told Kobe before a game the best way to score was not to try to score, he started playing that way, passing the ball whenever he could and he ended up scoring 16 points in the first quarter. Because he wasn't trying to score he was letting the game come to him. (Delahanty on Mumford in Mindful Magazine Feb 2016)

Martin Luther King also understood Wu Wei, as evidenced in the following quote:

> *If a man is called to be a street sweeper, he should sweep streets even as a Michelangelo painted, or Beethoven composed music or Shakespeare wrote poetry. He should sweep streets so well that all the hosts of heaven and earth will pause to say, 'Here lived a great street sweeper who did his job well. (Martin Luther King Jr. 1967)*

The art of Wu Wei and Not Doing is the unifying principle of life that springs from spontaneity and feels natural. We do our best and highest work in this mode.

No one can live in the state of Wu Wei all the time. Think of it as a natural park, much like Yosemite, Zion, or Yellowstone. By knowing this beautiful property exists we can visit there when we are most in need of correcting the imbalances in our life we have created. It is not a retreat but rather a fully immersed way of living by embracing and experiencing the ever–moving flow of life.

Sixteen

Mandala
A Picture of the Psyche

My mandalas were cryptograms concerning the state of the Self which was presented to me anew each day... I guarded them like precious pearls... It became increasingly plain to me that the mandala is the center. It is the exponent of all paths. It is the path to the center, to individuation. (Jung 1983)

The importance of the balancing and transcending of the opposites within our psyches cannot be stressed enough in the journey toward individuation.

Mandala is the ultimate symbol to work with in this process. The word Mandala comes from Sanskrit, the extinct language of ancient India, and means circle. In Jungian psychology it is the symbol of the Self, a picture of the psyche. It clearly fits the definition of

161

an archetype as a "particular, frequently occurring, formal aspect of instinct..." It existed as a form in many ancient cultures. Jung himself came upon it through his work and only later made the connection back to the mandalas of ancient China when Richard Wilhelm introduced him to *The Secret of the Golden Flower*. This further proved to him the connection between all cultures and times that lives in the ocean of the collective unconscious. He wrote "...I knew that in finding The mom "Darla" as an expression of the Self I had attained what was for me the ultimate. Perhaps someone else knows more, but not I. (Jung 1963)

In our lives we encounter mandala symbols everywhere. Slice an orange, an apple, or a kiwi in half and view a mandala. Look into the iris of an eye, the face of a flower, an astrological chart, the earth, a snowflake, a blood cell, a starfish, clocks, musical cymbals, and crop circles, a bicycle wheel, and the very egg that gave us life. All are mandalas. These are circular forms with a center that grows outward, often in a symmetrical pattern. It is the center that is the key that holds it together. Through his work Jung discovered that our growth psychically was not so much linear as it was rather more of a circumambulation throughout our lifetimes around our center, our Self.

Mandala used by Jung as a symbol of the psyche, is an extremely useful tool to glimpse that which is so often hidden from our view. It is like slicing and opening our mind in half.

A mandala can be as simple as a Native American teepee constructed around a center pole or as complex as their elaborate sand paintings, or the Mayan calendar, or the many stained-glass windows found in medieval European cathedrals.

A mandala as a tool reflects a moment in time. It offers a chance to see a picture of one's psyche in real time. It is interesting to me that with the advent of the digital camera, many of the photos we take are destined to live within the bowels of our computers and phones and never see the light of day. The impulse to take the picture represents the need to literally focus on a moment and just the act itself is satisfying.

This is how I view the mandala: whenever I am at odds with my Self, out of sorts, restless or in a state of conflict, I can find help by taking a picture of my psyche at that moment. It is a singularly meditative action.

Find a quiet place. Gather a pad of blank paper, a few colorful instruments such as markers, crayons, oil pastels, or watercolors and draw a circle. Give it a center in the form of a dot or small circle and begin by giving it your full attention. Use a dinner–sized plate, or any circular object to form the circle.

With your drawing instrument in hand follow whatever images and symbols come as you draw out from the center. Trust yourself. Spontaneity is everything. This is not graded or judged. If your ego is flinching at the idea of drawing and telling you that you cannot draw, you need to know that it is not your ego that is drawing; it is the Self that is expressing here. Your mandala may seem to be chaotic, filled to the edges, even spilling over, or it may be highly structured with equal, balanced proportions.

There are various types of mandala; the classical starts with a circular structure and is found in the eastern traditions.

The "squaring of the circle" is one of the most important of them portraying the archetype of wholeness. The four points of the square (the quaternity) is found as an archetype throughout the centuries as a religious symbol; the four seasons, the four points of the compass, and the four elements of earth, water, air and fire and others.

To follow a classical form, begin with the center and proceed to divide your mandala into four equal parts all arising from the center. The upper half can represent the conscious mind, heaven, light etc.; the lower can be the unconscious or hell, or darkness or any opposite. For every shape and color you put in one part, do the same in its opposite. This is a ritualistic form.

You may instead choose a second, more freeform way, more typical to our western culture. Experiment. The symbols you choose can be from your everyday world or from a more universal source. No two mandalas are ever the same, just as no moment in time is like any other. There is no right or wrong way. Allow ample time to sit with your circle. It is a container, which can hold all that is within you at that moment. The object is the Self at the center, not the ego, which can appear within the mandala but is not the focus. Jung called it "a safe refuge of inner reconciliation and wholeness." It was a major tool in his personal toolbox.

On a trip I took to his country home in Bollingen, Switzerland, I saw that he had carved mandalas into the stone walls of his patio. In his autobiography, Memories, Dreams, Reflections, Jung says "I sketched each morning in a small notebook, a small circular drawing, a mandala, which seemed to correspond to my situation at the time. With the help of these drawings I could observe my psychic transformations from day to day. Only gradually did I discover what the mandala really is... and that is the Self, the wholeness of the personality, which if all goes well is harmonious, but which cannot tolerate Self-deceptions."

Upon finishing your mandala you will have called upon all that you are in order to accomplish the act. Your hand did the physical act of drawing, your mind supplied the images, your feelings and intuition chose the colors that said it best, and the result is a snapshot of your 'whole' Self. It is a good idea to date your mandala for as you continue to make them certain patterns may appear. If you want you can name the mandala.

Amazing benefits occur as you sit with your mandala. You can meditate on the colors you chose as well as the shapes and what they mean to you. Think about each individual symbol and its place in your life. Does it parallel your life? Does it oppose your conscious attitude or conform to it? Devise your own questions to gain a deeper understanding. Write notes to yourself. How did you feel upon starting? How do you feel upon completion?

The most apparent and immediate benefit will be the awareness that whatever state of mind you were in at the approach now has moved and changed into something new in a way that your willpower alone can never achieve. This is the act of transcendence.

You can do a mandala to get at the root of a specific feeling such as fear, or love, loneliness or anger. You will discover how much more there is to know of these feelings than what you are conscious of. Attempt a mandala using your opposite hand for a new experience of yourself. Be free, experimental and enjoy the process.

Charles Gilchrist is a gifted mandala artist in Ohio who has had amazing results with the elderly suffering from dementia and Alzheimer's in his Ennis Court Mandala project. The results can be viewed at Ennis Court Mandala Project.com

Ennis Court is a home for the elderly in Lakewood, Ohio, and the project involves having the residents create a mandala. In this way they are connecting to parts of themselves otherwise lost.

Create an album of your mandala art, as you would a photo album, although this album displays the pictures of your psyche and provides a way to connect to your inner Self.

And then there is the living mandala. Placing myself in the center of my home I take a 360° look. I see how I have unfolded my true Self within these walls and this space. When I look at this mandala with a clear vision, I can see that there is room for the clutter and the order, the flaws and the perfection. Here I connect to the circle of my community, within the circle of my town, within the circle of my country, within the circle of my world, within the circle of my universe.

Seventeen

Synchronicity

Meaningful Coincidence

It is difficult for many twenty-first century, rational, technological and rather egocentric beings, to grasp the idea of coincidence as meaningful and to give it credit for any real role in our lives. This was not the case for Jung for whom coincidences became another form of expression of conscious and unconscious communication of needs, desires and meaning. He called this phenomenon synchronicity. For all those in today's world who feel lonely, disconnected, alienated, and unaware that they are part of a larger picture, synchronistic events can shape perception and act as the connecting glue.

An awareness of synchronicity in action can come when events occur that are totally unexpected and unplanned and yet become most meaningful. There are times when our life and another person's coincide and resonate in ways that seem impossible or at the least highly improbable. And yet as we progress we see that these so-called accidental happenings have great meaning and impact on our lives, that our meeting of others are not nearly as accidental as one may at first think.

In the eastern world the word for the connecting glue is Tao. Jung tells of his friend Wm. McDougall who asked a Chinese student of his "What exactly do you mean by Tao?" The Chinese student explained what Tao is and McDougall replied: "I do not understand yet." The Chinese student went out to the balcony and said, "What do you see?"

"I see a street and houses and people walking and tramcars passing."

"What more?"

"There is a hill."

"What more?"

"Trees."

"What more?

"The wind is blowing."

The Chinese threw up his arms and said, "That is Tao."

Jung says, "There you are. Tao can be anything. I use another word to designate it but it is poor enough. I call it synchronicity. It is like this: you are standing on the seashore and the waves wash up an old hat, an old box, a shoe, and a dead fish and there they lie on the shore. You say: 'Chance, nonsense!' But for the Chinese mind nothing is random and the specific array of objects, events or even people at specific moments in time may provide insights or a window onto what is taking place or what is about to occur." As Jung says "The Chinese mind experiments with that being together and coming together at the right moment and it has an experimental method which is not well known in the west, but which plays a large role in the philosophy of the East. This method...is the I- Ching."

The I-Ching is an ancient Chinese text that greatly influenced Eastern philosophy throughout history. Possibly the oldest book in the world, it is a philosophical system whose roots lie in the concept of Ying and Yang. Its eloquent writings are filled with wisdom and guidance that even though ancient in origin are timeless.

The I-Ching is composed of 64 hexagrams each with its own symbolic meaning. The lines are determined by a series of six broken or solid lines divided into two groups of three lines each called a trigram. The lines within each hexagram are stacked one on top of each other and read from the bottom up.

The hexagram is formed by the throwing of three coins or the more ancient yarrow stalks. Some of the lines become changing lines and form entirely new hexagrams in response to your question. Change, chance and wisdom are the inherent attributes of the I Ching.

I was introduced to the I-Ching during my Jungian analysis. I continue to use this tool whenever I am entirely stuck between two opposing positions and cannot make a decision. There is a great deal of wisdom found here and after I have consulted it in a serious way I am always able to break the bind. It is not fortune telling but rather a practical guide to life.

By the early 1920s Jung was already familiar with the I-Ching, also called the Book of Changes. He ended up through a series of his own chance happenings to write the introduction in the most accessible English translation, The Wilhelm, Baynes edition. In this introduction he writes:

> *The Chinese mind, as I see it at work in the I-Ching, seems to be exclusively preoccupied with the chance aspect of events... We must admit that there is something to be said for the immense importance of chance...While the Western mind carefully sifts, weighs, selects, classifies, and isolates, the Chinese picture of the moment, which the I-Ching presents, encompasses everything down to the minutest nonsensical detail, because all the ingredients make up the observed moment...*

I have had many experiences of synchronicity or meaningful coincidence in my life since becoming aware that such was possible. One of the best examples combined the tool of the dream with the tool of synchronicity to affect one of the most significant events in my life. When I look back it could not have been any other way.

Before my husband and I were married, we needed to find a home that would be located centrally for both of us, since each day we headed off in two different directions. It was really a problem and seemed to be preventing our marriage. One night I had a dream: I was driving on a specific freeway and when I looked off to my left there was a beautiful green hill with houses on it. I got off of the freeway and found the hill. When I drove to the top I entered a wonderful sunlit neighborhood and there on top of the hill was a house for sale.

When I woke from this dream, I felt like a person with a mission. I called my husband-to-be and told him my dream and that I felt I had to take the same trip on the freeway and see if such a place existed. I did just that. Soon I saw the hill, one I had passed very often, but this time I took the off-ramp leading to the top.

I was literally astounded as I entered what appeared to be a small village. This in the middle of Los Angeles. The sun was out and all the homes were well maintained, with lovely gardens. I quickly found a phone and told my fiancé what I had found.

The next day he joined me and as we drove through the neighborhood loving it more and more, we saw a man putting a "For Sale" sign in front of a house on the top of the hill. We bought it. It has been our home together and it has been the warmest home I have ever known. We call it our "dream" home. Many synchronistic events have happened to me since living here. It resulted in a complete change of my business - all for the better - an amazing group of neighbors who have become close friends, and it led me to the community of artists I have been part of for the last twenty years. I cannot imagine what my life would have been without this move.

This is "synchronicity" at work. It is also the value and power of the dream which often is the vehicle for bringing chance to our lives.

Every time you receive a call from someone you have just thought of, you are experiencing synchronicity. Sometimes that call or visit just reinforces a deep bond that we have in this lifetime with that person. Other times it can lead to a completely new life path or set of experiences. Sometimes these synchronistic events are associated with opportunities or openings that can improve our emotional or spiritual or financial lives.

I am writing this chapter in a studio at the beach and it the "just right" place to do this work. I needed to get away, by myself, with no telephones, or distractions of any kind. I did not know where to go and was telling my problem to my friend, Dianne, when we collided in a synchronistic way. She said, "Oh, I'm leaving town and I would be thrilled if you would come and stay at my place and water my plants while I'm gone." Her place is this perfect hideaway that is nourishing me so I may do my work.

In another example the use of the I-Ching provided me a perfect solution to timing a business transaction. For a short time my fiancé and I owned a small Laundromat. All was going well until we left for a week to get married in another state. My cousin agreed to help with the simple tasks of collecting coins and wiping down the machines. The night before our wedding I received the call. Our boiler burst, flooding adjoining businesses in the strip mall we were part of. It became a nightmare and we considered selling. It was November. When we arrived back home, we were still undecided and so we consulted the I-Ching. The reading we received in answer to our question, "should we sell," was hexagram #21 Biting Through. In the reading the months April and May were referenced. This implied to us to "bite through" and continue to improve the Laundromat, by making. needed repairs. That pretty much decided us to wait until spring. One April day I was washing down the machines when a young man walked in, asked if I was the owner and asked if I was interested in selling.

We signed the papers that night. That is synchronicity in action.

> *Synchronistic* experiences give us the certain knowledge that we are not alone" and that who we are, how we are connected and what we do are not random. "This is why these events are often felt as numinous, religious, or spiritual experiences. (Jung)

Walking down a hall in my office building feeling sorry for myself because my sinuses were bothering me, a spastic, crippled young man struggled past me, made his way to the elevator and smiled at me. He became my synchronistic gift for the day. Why was this synchronistic? I immediately stopped my self-pitying attitude. My whole day changed for the better.

Lockhart, In *Psyche Speaks,* tells of being asked if he could capture the essence of Jung's psychology in a single phrase. After waiting for his intuition to click in, he said, "Everything belongs." That is the spirit of synchronicity. Everything does belong, including each of us. Once we develop the way of being that looks for the meaning and connectedness of all things, we can begin to feel ourselves becoming connected to the oneness and the wonder of it all. This in turn fills us with the wonderful sense of being part of some larger or more comprehensive universe.

Part Three

Closing

Eighteen

Transformation

The Transcendent Function

Since life cannot tolerate a standstill, a damning up of vital energy results, and this would lead to an insupportable condition did not the tension of the opposites produce a new, uniting function that transcends them. This function is the transcendent function.(Jung 1963)

When you reach the point of having found the properties of the unconscious you're still left to do negotiation for the development phase before you can truly take ownership and develop a new attitude. Ownership (awareness) of the unconscious properties/archetypes and the conscious attitudes are only stepping-stones on the path to Individuation. The next step is a transition that signals a change in which a new property is developed, a property that transcends the others and shines as a brand new way of being, complete with new attitudes. This is the transcendent function, which Jung said lies at the heart of Individuation.

In 1893 Russian author Leo Tolstoy wrote the passage below in *The Kingdom Of God is Within You*. The book was banned in Russia but published in Germany in 1984. I think he spoke of a time when the transcendent function was needed in his own life.

> *Whether the former, habitual conditions of life will be retained, whether they will be destroyed, or whether entirely new ones, better ones, will arise. It is inevitably necessary to leave the old conditions of our life, which have become impossible and pernicious, and to go ahead and meet the future conditions. (Tolstoy 1893)*

We may encounter the need for the transcendent function when our life feels as though it is at a stand still. Like a dam holding back the floodwaters, our conscious mind may have turned its back on our unconscious and is saying "no" to its counterpart property seeking entry. The fact is neither aspect, conscious or unconscious, should win out because both are a part of who we really are. Instead we need to reconcile them so that they birth a new transformed part of us, not a combination, but an actual new third entity.

We can witness transcendence in the world we live in where rustic environments and completely urban environments have transcended to become suburban environments. The day and the night transcend into dawn and dusk. Cold and hot become warm, lightning is created from negative energy colliding with positive. Human population is experiencing massive transcendence. My neighbor's beautiful grandchildren are blended combinations of Irish, Indian, Japanese and Hispanic. The day may come when we no longer identify as a specific race or ethnicity.

During my career in Real Estate I have observed that in all the areas where I have sold homes, there is always an invisible border. The differences may appear subtle but are very clear to those living there. As a kid I grew up on the wrong side, literally, of the tracks since our house was directly across from an elevated train track. On our side lived poor, lower middle class, blue-collar workers. Our area consisted of narrow streets, small lots with bare bones houses that we were glad to own because further east of us there were those who were worse off. We had a liquor store on the corner and a small convenience store for a carton of milk, a loaf of bread and a pack of cigarettes. For my purposes here I will call this the unconscious for it was a forgotten neighborhood, invisible if you will.

Just a few short miles away on the other side of the tracks existed the good side of town with well-to-do people living on wide tree-lined streets, in beautiful brick homes, with private schools, and great shopping and pretty much oblivious to those of us on the other side. Let's call this the conscious side.

When I began to get into trouble with my friends on my side of town, my parents wanted me to mingle with people of "better ilk" and they got me into a religious club with girls that were all from the "good" side.

Just as the unconscious contains all that is opposite to the conscious mind, my two sides of town couldn't have been more opposite. At first I remained an outsider. My clothes were all hand me downs. These girls wore cashmere sweaters and Murray Bender loafers, the rage at the time. The soles of my shoes were stuck together with chewing gum. But then, being the extroverted, intuitive, and feeling kind of person that I am naturally, I couldn't stay quiet for long. Slowly, I made friends. As time passed and as we got to know each other independent of the stereotypes, I was no longer the girl from the wrong side of the tracks and they were no longer the snooty upper-class girls I thought they were. We actually became friends.

To me this is what Jung meant by the Transcendent function. Because when the opposites that exist as properties in our unconscious enter into dialogue with its opposite in our conscious minds, through our dreams or other connecting symbols, a totally new entity comes into being. This third entity is the one long sought after by the Self and which transforms us and allows us to become closer to the individuated, whole person, we are meant to be.

Jung concerned himself with the transcendence we experience on our soul's journey to wholeness. When we have become aware of our unconscious contents we then need to find a way to bridge these opposites to our conscious minds and integrate them into our personalities as an entirely new function. This third new attitude now allows us the full access to our whole selves, having found, owned, and developed many of the archetypes/properties that have been waiting to become available to use in our lives. We have differentiated our conscious functions of thinking, feeling, intuition, and sensation which are now available to us and make the interpretation of our life events much more rich and accurate. We have partnered with Anima, Animus, and learned to access wisdom. The once scary, unwanted shadow parts of our psyches are now welcome neighbors. Creating this new neighborhood is the heart of Individuation.

In a recent dream of mine, two me's, one white, one black, are riding in bumper cars, gently nudging each other. Soon the bumper cars merge and become one with just one of me, now the color of latte. What has happened? The new latte-colored one is neither white nor black but a new third choice. At the time of the dream I didn't know what I was integrating into my life. But through other dreams to follow I discovered a new feminine aspect I had not previously accepted, being a modern 21st century business woman, rational, decisive, and with a strong animus identification. I was not acknowledging, or letting into consciousness a softer, more vulnerable me, who allows others to cross the moat to my heart.

As a result, as I integrate these two opposite aspects, each is producing in me a third and new kind of woman who can be soft and feminine but still capable and assertive. But most of all my heart is opening in an honest and completely new way to those around me.

There is a certain amount of trepidation that goes with this time of transcendence and integration, both individual and collective. That is as it should be but it can become anxiety producing. "It can rock your world" as my Jungian analyst says. I have been on shaky ground because the known is slipping away and the unknown is looming. A symbol is often the mediator. For me it is the new latte colored woman in a bumper car. Transcendence takes courage.

Since this dream I am much more aware of any new behaviors that I may be exhibiting as they are becoming more natural. As well, I am conscious of ways of being that no longer serve me and one by one I am letting them go. I don't claim that this is easy but I already sense rewards. The biggest change is that as I become more authentic the response from others has changed. By being more emotionally available and true to my Self, even my already good husband of thirty plus years has opened up more to me. Perhaps through transcendence I have created a safer space "for me and for thee."

Nineteen

Individuation

While all paths in this book and Jung's psychology lead to Individuation, it is increasingly hard to come by in the egocentric times in which we live. Celebrity reigns supreme and it is discouraging that for many young people their goal in life is "to be famous."

The word entitlement is today in common usage. Many young people are described as "feeling entitled". Millennials are often referred to as the Entitlement generation. The good news is that studies have shown that feelings of entitlement do diminish with age.

The definition of entitled is granting or awarding title. In real estate "Title" is the proof of ownership of your properties. One may feel entitled and wait their whole life to receive rewards they think should come to them, then end up disappointed and with little to show for a lifetime of waiting but having never found, owned, or developed their inner properties. But if we can put our egos aside, we come to see that the only true Title we each have an absolute right and ability to obtain is Title to the whole person we were born to be.

For Jung, "The privilege of a lifetime is to become who you truly are."

A completely individuated person would look a lot like Jesus or Buddha, or other such spiritual beings imbued with the powers of God. My image of individuation as a property is a light-filled energetic body of pure wisdom. We would know all, see all and be all. Jung said "Individuation is a philosophical, spiritual and mystical experience. It is the goal of our psychological development and in metaphysical terms it amounts to God's incarnation."

There exist, of course, egos, which go through life with this false, fixed belief but to actually become individuated the ego would have long ago surrendered its position as number one. I think of individuation as the graduation from university. You have majored in property acquisitions and you have received a PhD in life. I love what Jung said an analyst should do:

> Therefore, anyone who wants to know the human psyche would be better advised to bid farewell to his study and wander with human heart through the world. There, in the horrors of prisons, lunatic asylums, some hospitals, in drab suburban pubs, in brothels, in gambling halls, in the salons of the elegant, the stock

exchanges, socialist meetings, churches, revivalist gatherings and ecstatic sects, through love and hate, through the experience of passion in every form in his own body, he would reap richer stores of knowledge than textbooks a foot thick could give him, and he will know how to doctor the sick with real knowledge of the human soul. (Jung 1916)

Of course we are not likely to experience all of the above, but it speaks to experiencing our own lives in the fullest way possible by not shrinking from the dark side and not resisting the unfamiliar, the inner messages from our unconscious. Becoming receptive to all that our Self is asking of us and joyfully applying the lessons of life allows the full experience of life.

If we successfully individuate we have made the heroic journey, slain our dragons or at the very least acknowledged them as the protectors of our Self rather than the enemy. By having owned and developed the inner properties and now having become the separate, truly individual human being we were born to be with all elements of our personalities integrated, we can consciously put on whatever "mask" is needed for the situation we are in and no one mask is stuck to us permanently. We have rescued and made friends with the parts of ourselves we previously disowned and relegated to the shadow.

As a man your Anima is your treasured ally who has given you the ability to be receptive to the qualities of your soul, aiding you in all relationships and creativity. As a woman our animus is no longer controlling us but instead is now our faithful partner in life, giving courage, independence and strength.

The Wise Old Woman and the Wise Old Man have become our special partners aiding in all decision making and helping to guide those in our charge in the ways of the world. We are now teachers as well as continuing students. Individuation is completely inclusive of all that we are. The division between the conscious world and the unconscious is no longer a solid wall but instead a thin and transparent veil we can easily pass through.

I was struck recently after the death of Muhammad Ali by the thought that here was a fully individuated human being. All the stories that followed his death revealed the depth of his character. He knew who he was and what he was here to do and he didn't preach it, he lived it. We saw the true Self shine through his many adversities as well as times of good fortune. Even suffering with Parkinson's for thirty years he used his illness to keep growing as he saw it as an opportunity for learning and continued giving. We saw in him a whole person who developed through all the ups and downs of his life right before our eyes.

On the complete opposite spectrum, another man from a poor background, also blessed with amazing athletic abilities and the gift of charm, this man, O.J. Simpson, let his Ego only lead his way in life and now sits in jail. The documentary of O.J.'s life came out the same week in 2016 that Ali was memorialized and the differences in the outcomes of their lives stand out to me in a most meaningful way.

The good news is that our life spans are ever growing longer and while they still may not be long enough to reach full individuation, we are privileged to have years more to plumb the depths and work toward our becoming Self-realized individuals. The process itself becomes the worthy goal for our lives.

Twenty

The Self

Jung believed the ego to be the center of our conscious minds while the Self is the center of the total personality which includes ego, consciousness and the unconscious and to him our return to the Self, from which we sprang, is the ultimate goal of life.

He postulated that we are born whole but as our egos develop and emerge during the first half of our lives we soon are positioned firmly in the outer world, while at the same time this process has distanced us from our originating and whole Self. As we age, therefore, we need to seek Individuation, which is the final step to reunion with our Self. By working with the properties presented in this book you can begin the journey.

1. Through the discovery of our Shadow we open the first door to the Self since as the home of the discarded aspects of our personality, we must find and

own those discounted properties as the first step in the process of our individuation.

2. Next in our reconnection to Self come the encounters with our Anima/Animus, perfect mediators "between our consciousness and unconsciousness and able representatives of the Self." (Jung 1962)

3.The final bridge to the property of the Self comes from the Wisdom figures, Wise Old Man/Woman, as archetypes of The Collective Unconscious and the nearest neighbor of all to the Self. (Jung 1962)

Taking ownership of our wisdom properties will lead us to the doorstep of the property of the Self. How do we know when we have owned these wisdom properties? For me it is all about awareness. I am now aware when my Ego is trying to control my actions and I consciously pull back. When dark and negative voices tell me how bad I am I stop and consciously converse with them to see what they want. When my animus wants to possess me I find a creative way to let him into my life. In other words I am living life with my wisdom properties when I stay aware of what I am doing and reject those things that keep me from making the most of my time on earth and my relationships to the people in my life and my community.

Jung believed this rediscovery and connection to the Self is our task for the second half of life. This need grows more intense in our midlife. Once connected we are able to accept life not as we wish it to be but rather as it is. This acceptance can bring enormous peace.

I once had a client who had been reluctantly removed from her childhood home, so much so that when the home was up for sale, she took the "For Sale" signs down on a daily basis. She had never fully recovered from her early loss. Years later, now a grown woman, I was assisting her in finding a home. Nothing measured up to her memories of her childhood home. Then in a breath-taking synchronicity, that childhood home came on the market. Needless to say she bought it. Her joy was palpable as we found her five-year-old handprints and her dogs paw prints embedded in the cement patio.

Her search has stayed with me as a metaphorical reminder of the search for the Self, our first home that lies patiently in wait for all of us as we traverse the ups and downs of our lives. This search often arises and begins in earnest as the result of a psychic wounding, or a serious life crisis, usually in midlife.

But this is not an "as the crow flies" journey from birth to death. Jung said:

> *...Between 1918 and 1920, I begin to understand that the goal of psychic development is the Self. There is no linear evolution; there is only a circumambulation of the Self. Uniform development exists, at most, only at the beginning; later, everything points toward the center. This insight gave me stability, and gradually my inner peace returned. (Jung 1965)*

Indeed, I have found my journey to Individuation and reunion with my Self, to be a circular one. I see myself as an orbiting planet that gets a little closer to its sun with each pass. I have encountered my shadow, my animus and my wisdom partners over and over again and each encounter brings me deeper as I circle my Self. Every time I face a new crisis or challenge in life, I make contact again and strive to integrate my unconscious into consciousness. I do this in order to awake the transcendent function so I may be open to a new attitude that can move me to reunite with the Self and the person I was meant to be at birth, before life's conditions altered me. And whether or not I ever become a fully Self-realized person at the end of my life, the search, the inner work, the awareness that the journey brings to me, allows me - an ordinary woman - to live an extraordinary life. I wish you all a...

Bon Voyage!

About the Author

Joanne Park was born in Cleveland Ohio. She attended Ohio University in Athens Ohio before moving to Hermosa Beach in Southern California in the early 60's where she continued studies at UCLA, El Camino College, Santa Monica College and Los Angeles City College. She proceeded to gather life experience through twenty-six diverse jobs until she entered the real estate profession, becoming an owner/ broker of her own firm until the present day. All the while pursuing her interests in writing, painting and Jungian studies. She participated in many classes at the Jung Institute in Los Angeles, as well as taking "A journey into the unconscious" to Zurich Switzerland where she attended classes, visited Jung's birthplace in Basel, his home in Bollingen and met many intimates in Jung's life. She resides in Los Angeles with her husband Ken, a percussionist/drummer, whose music career has taken them on travels throughout the world.

Permissions

In relation to books, articles, websites and all other forms of copyrighted materials, the authors have followed the fair use policy as outlined by Chicago University press. For police copyright and fair use policies please refer to

http://www.Press.uchicago.edu/Misc/ Chicago/copy-and-perms.pdf

Works Cited

Bly, Robert. *A little Book On The Human Shad*ow. Wm. Booth Ed. Harper Collins ,Publisher. 1988

Briggs, Myers. Personality Test. On-line

Cousins, Norman. *Anatomy of an Illness.* W.W. Norton company, 2005.

Harding, Esther. *The Way Of All Women.* Harpern colophon Books, 1970.

I-Ching. Wilhelm Baynes Edition. Forward by C.G.Jung.Bollingen Series XIX Princeton. Princeton University Press.1974

Jacobe, Jolanda. *The Way Of Individuation.*

Jaffe, Aniela. *The Myth of Meaning.* Penguin Books, 1975The Myth of Meaning.

Johnson, Robert. I*nner Work* Harper One, 2009

Jung, C.G. *Aspects of the Feminine* Trans. R.F.C.Hull.From C.W. vol 6,7,9,10,17.Bollingen Series XX . Princeton.Princeton University Press.

Jung, C.G. "Basel Seminar." Basel, 1934.

Jung, C.G. etal. *Collected Works.* Bollingen Series XX. Edited by G, McGuire Wm. Read,H. Fordham,M Adler.

Translated by Hull R.F.C. 20 vols. Princeton, New Jersey: Princeton University Press, 1973.

Jung, C.G. Freud, Sigmond. *The Freud/Jung Letters.* Edited by William Mcguire. Princeton, New Jersey: Princeton University Press, 1974.

Jung, C.G. *Man and his Symbols,.* Edited by John Jung C.G.,von Franz M.L. Freeman. New York: Aldus Books, 1964.

Jung, C.G. *Memories, Dreams, Reflections.* New York: Doubleday, 1965.

—. *Symbols of the Unconscious.* Edited by John Freeman. New York: Doubleday, 1964.

Jung, Carl. *Psychological Types.* Princeton/Bollingen. Vol. 6. Princeton, New Jersey, 1921.

Jung. C.G. *Symbols of Transformation.* Trans. R.F.C. Hull.Vol 5 C.W. Princeton. Princeton University Press

Keirsey, David. *Please Understand Me.* Green Valley, Ca. Prometheus Nemisis Books.1984

Lockhart, Russell Arthur. *Psyche Speaks.* Wilmette, Illinois: Chiron Publishing, 1987.

McGuire, and R F C Hull. *C.G.Jung Speaking.* Princeton , New Jersey: Princeton University Press, 1977.

George Mumford, author of *The Mindful Athlete, The Secrets to Pure Performance,*

Patterson, Charles. *Anti-Semitism- The Holocaust and Beyond.*

R.F., McGuire Wm. & Hull. *C.G. Jung Speaking.* . Bollingen. Princeton: Princeton University Press, 1977.

Sanford, John A. *The Invisible Partners.* New York: Paulist Press, 1980.

Secret of the Golden Flower. Trans Richard Wilhelm. Commentary C.G.Jung. Harcourt Brace & Co. San Diego. 1962

Shalit, Erel. *The Hero and his Shadow.* University Press Of America, 2003.

von Franz, Maria. *Archetypal Dimensions of the Psyche.* Shambala. Boston Mass: Shambala, 1997.

von Franz, Marie Louise. *Psychotheraoy.* Boston, Mass: Shambala, 2001.

vonFranz. *Anima,Animus.* Vol. 7. Princeton , New Jersey: Princeton University Press.

Bibliography

Campbell, Joseph. *An Open Life.* Conversation with Michael Toms. New York, Harper & Row, Publishers. 1989

Campbell, Joseph. *Myths To Live By* Viking Edition. Bantam Books. Toronto 1972

Cousins, Norman. *Anatomy of an Illness.* W.W. Norton company, 2005.

Harding, M. Esther. *the i and the not i.* Bollingen Series. Princeton. Princeton University Press. *1964*

Harding, M. Esther. *The Way Of All Women.* Harpern colophon Books, 1970.

I-Ching. Wilhelm Baynes Edition. Forward by C.G.Jung.Bollingen Series XIX Princeton. Princeton University Press.1974

Jacobe, Jolanda. *The Way Of Individuation.*

Jaffe, Aniela. *The Myth of Meaning.* Penguin Books, 1975The Myth of Meaning.

Jung, C.G. *Aspects of the Feminine* Trans. R.F.C.Hull.From C.W. vol 6,7,9,10,17.Bollingen Series XX . Princeton. Princeton University Press.

Jung, C.G. "Basel Seminar." Basel, 1934.

Jung, C.G. etal. *Collected Works.* Bollingen Series XX. Edited by G, McGuire Wm. Read,H. Fordham,M Adler. Translated by Hull R.F.C. 20 vols. princeton, new jersey: Princeton University Press, 1973.

Jung, C.G. *Dreams.* New York MJF Books 1974

Jung, C.G. Freud, Sigmond. *The Freud/Jung Letters.* Edited by William Mcguire. Princeton, New Jersey: Princeton University Press, 1974.

Jung, C.G. *Man and his Symbols,.* Edited by John Jung C.G.,von Franz M.L. Freeman. New York: Aldus Books, 1964.

Jung, Carl Gustav. A Memorial Meeting. The Analytical psychology club of New York 1961

Jung, C.G.. *Memories, Dreams, Reflections.* new york: Doubleday, 1965.

Jung. C.G. *Modern Man in Search of a Soul.* New York Harcourt, Brace & World, Inc. 1933.

Jung. C.G. *Symbols of Transformation.* Trans. R.F.C. Hull.Vol 5 C.W. Princeton. Princeton University Press

—. *Symbols of the Unconscious.* Edited by John Freeman. New York: Doubleday, 1964.

Jung, Carl. *Psychological Types.* Princeton/Bollingen. Vol. 6. Princeton, New Jersey, 1921.

Lockhart, Russell Arthur. *Psyche Speaks.* Wilmette, Illinois: Chiron Publishing, 1987.

McGuire, and R F C Hull. *C.G.Jung Speaking.* Princeton , New Jersey: Princeton University Press, 1977.

Patterson, Chsrles. *Anti-Semitism- The Holocaust and Beyond.*

R.F., McGuire Wm. & Hull. *C.G. Jung Speaking.* . Bollingen. Princeton: Princeton University Press, 1977.

Sandford, John A. *Dreams and Healing.* New York.Paulist Press 1978

Sanford, John A. *The Invisible Partners.* New York: Paulist Press, 1980.

Secret of the Golden Flower. Trans Richard Wilhelm. Commentary C.G.Jung. Harcourt Brace & Co. San Diego. 1962

Shalit, Erel. *The Hero and his Shadow.* University Press Of America, 2003.

Von Franz, Maria. *Archetypal Dimensions of the Psyche.* Shambala. Boston Mass: Shambala, 1997.

von Franz, Marie- Louise. *Psychotheraoy.* Boston, Mass: Shambala, 2001.

vonFranz. Marie-Louise. *Anima,Animus.* Vol. 7. Princeton , New Jersey: Princeton University Press.

von Franz, Marie-Louise; *The Interpretations Of Fairy Tales.* Boulder. Shambala 1996

*Last but not least the amazing *Red Book* by C.G Jung - an intricate 16 year journey into his unconscious, described as an extraordinary book of science and work of art. Edited and Introduced by Sonu Shamdasani. The heirs of C.G.Jung and the Philemon Society 2009

Appendix

List of possible Archetypes
Goodgirl/goodboy; thief; miser; rescuer; clown; rebel;orphan; coward; virgin; homeless one; beggar; shape shifter; caretaker; bully; politicians; athlete; prince; queen; advocate; princess; poet; the one who hides; student; hero/heroine; martyr; mother; father; shaman; pioneer; fool; puppet; trickster; nag; critic; organizer; intellectual; diva; nun; eternal child; healer; prostitute; visionary; scientist; goddess; professor; angel; messiah; negotiator; wise woman; teacher; wise man; vagabond; puritan; seeker; storyteller.

Jung's Twenty Volume Collected Works
Volume 1: Psychiatric Studies
Volume 2: Experimental Researches
Volume 3: Psychogenesis of Mental Disease
Volume 4: Freud & Psychoanalysis
Volume 5: Symbols of Transformation
Volume 6: Psychological Types
Volume 7: Two Essays in Analytical Psychology
Volume 8: Structure & Dynamics of the Psyche
Volume 9:(1): Archetypes and the Collective Unconscious
Volume 9:(2): Aion: Researches into Phenomenology of the Self
Volume 10: Civilization in Transition
Volume 11: Psychology and Religion: West and East
Volume 12: Psychology and Alchemy
Volume 13: Alchemical Studies

Volume 14: Mysterium Conjunctionis
Volume 15: Spirit in Man, Art, And Literature.
Volume16: Practice of Psychotherapy
Volume17: Development of personality
Volume18:The symbolic life
Volume 19: Complete bibliography
Volume 20: Collected works digital.

Made in the USA
Middletown, DE
05 November 2019

78011821R00128